Monetary Policy and Its Unintended Consequences

T0292788

Monetary Policy and Its Unintended Consequences

Raghuram Rajan

The MIT Press
Cambridge, Massachusetts
London, England

The MIT Press would like to thank the anonymous peer reviewers who provided comments on drafts of this book. The generous work of academic experts is essential for establishing the authority and quality of our publications. We acknowledge with gratitude the contributions of these otherwise uncredited readers.

This book was set in Stone Serif and Stone Sans by Westchester Publishing Services. Printed and bound in the United States of America.

Library of Congress Cataloging-in-Publication Data is available.

ISBN: 978-0-262-54704-8

10 9 8 7 6 5 4 3

Contents

Series Foreword

The Swiss National Bank is grateful to Raghuram Rajan for writing this book, in which he revisits and develops the ideas presented in his Karl Brunner Lecture of 19 September 2019. The series of books associated with the Karl Brunner Distinguished Lecture explores topics of key importance to central banking.

The Karl Brunner Distinguished Lecture Series, which is organized by the Swiss National Bank and takes place annually in Zurich, honors eminent monetary theory and policy thinkers whose research has influenced central banking. The scope of the lecture reflects the attention Karl Brunner devoted to monetary economics, his belief in the need to advance theoretical and applied analysis in this field, and in particular his concern for the policy relevance of economic science.

Thomas J. Jordan, Chairman of the Governing Board

Introduction: Monetary Policy and Its Unintended Consequences

Karl Brunner was a great monetary economist as well as a prolific institution builder, founding such venerable institutions as the Shadow Open Market Committee, the *Journal of Money, Credit and Banking*, and the *Journal of Monetary Economics*. He was also a critic of central bank practice. So when the Swiss National Bank asked me to deliver the 2019 Karl Brunner Lecture, I knew what I wanted to speak about: the unintended consequences of monetary policy, especially in its more recent and unorthodox forms.

My research interests in banking and liquidity had always drawn me to issues of financial instability, but in August 2005, I became very concerned about the real-world consequences. I was giving a talk at the annual central bankers' meeting at Jackson Hole. This one was special for it was the last conference for Alan Greenspan as the chairman of the Federal Reserve. I tried to join in the spirit of celebration, but I could not, for I worried about the tail risks that were building up in the financial system. In particular, I pointed to the perverse incentives for private players to take risk in an environment of low rates.[1] It was no comfort to me when these risks were realized during the Global Financial Crisis (GFC).

But as central banks embarked on yet more accommodative and even unorthodox policies to revive economies that had been laid low by the crisis, I worried that we were ignoring a prime cause of the crisis—the role of central banks themselves. Indeed, now that private players and markets had proven wanting, it seemed as if there were no limits on what central bankers could, or should, do. They intervened merrily in a variety of markets, supporting prices and sometimes market players. They occasionally tied monetary policy actions to market movements and sentiments. And focusing on domestic inflation and real activity, they paid insufficient heed to the consequence of their actions on systemic leverage, financial instability, and spillovers to other countries.

Somewhat perversely, the more the central bank did, the more it was expected to do, and the more it ended up doing. Despite all the Federal Reserve's prior interventions, financial markets were still fragile when the 2020 pandemic hit. The Fed not only brought out the toolkit it had put together for the GFC—ironically, termed a once-in-a-century event when it occurred—but also added new measures. Today, partly because of the extraordinary fiscal response to the pandemic, inflation has started rearing its head. Central banks now have to combat inflation in economies that are not used to higher policy interest rates and where markets scarcely believe central banks will impose them.

It is not clear how all this will end. As I write this introductory note, two mid-sized banks have failed in the United States, all depositors have implicitly become insured by the government, the Fed has agreed to accept eligible securities as collateral at face value, and one large bank has been forcibly merged in Europe with the help of government guarantees. Regardless of how we muddle through, the central argument in this book is that monetary adventurism is rarely as much of a panacea as we think and often has unintended effects. It is therefore a plea to central bankers that they return to being conservative and boring and not assume they have the answers to every economic problem. The appeal is one that I think Karl Brunner would endorse.

The first chapter of this book is a lightly edited inaugural Andrew Crockett Memorial Lecture that I gave at the Bank for International Settlements (BIS) in June 2013, a few months before I took over as the governor of the Reserve Bank of India. In May 2013, Fed Chairman Bernanke had announced a likely taper to quantitative easing. The announcement precipitated rapid capital flight from emerging markets. India was one of the countries experiencing the "taper tantrum," and I was at the Ministry of Finance, helping to coordinate our response. In the Andrew Crockett Lecture, I surveyed some of the reasons for the adoption of unconventional monetary policies after the GFC. I worried that the underlying problems were more structural than cyclical and beyond the ambit of monetary policy solutions—a version of what Larry Summers later termed "secular stagnation." Nevertheless, central bankers had sallied forth into the breach. The adverse cross-border spillovers, reaped by emerging markets around the world, were a consequence.

In chapter 2, a heavily edited version of my 2018 Mundell Fleming lecture at the International Monetary Fund (IMF), I offer a sketch of a model describing how monetary policy spillovers can cause leveraging, booms, and eventually busts in capital-receiving countries. The model is primarily a corporate finance model, reinterpreted to accommodate a role for capital flows and exchange rate movements.

Recognizing that core country monetary policies affect countries at the periphery, often in a manner that is not to their choosing or their benefit, I ask in chapter 3 how one might begin thinking about what rules might be necessary to constrain core country monetary policies—and what research and debate might be needed to develop a consensus about these rules. This is an edited version of a paper with Prachi Mishra of the IMF, a longstanding colleague in organizations across the world. In this era of increasing global frictions, it might seem naive to propose global rules. Yet it is precisely when there is a lot of suspicion about the motives of other countries that it might make sense to start discussing rules of the new monetary game—after all the rules embedded in the post–World War II global order were essential to dispel distrust among countries, distrust engendered by a world war, and the prewar beggar-thy-neighbor economic strategies followed by countries. Of course, there is no global hegemon today with the heft of the immediate postwar United States that can bring conflicting parties together, but we must try.

Chapter 4 is a lightly edited version of a talk I gave at the Cato Institute's Annual Monetary Conference in 2021. I return to the issues I addressed in the first chapter, after the passage of nearly a decade. Perhaps I am inflexible and incorrigible, or perhaps I am on the side of the angels here. At any rate, I still believe that, as with most actions, monetary policy is best conducted with moderation and with humility about the unintended consequences of policy.

I end the book with an update based on recent developments, reiterating the case for a focused central bank mandate—combating high inflation while keeping an eye on financial stability.

Intellectually, I have benefited tremendously from the work of Claudio Borio and Hyun Song Shin at the Bank of International Settlements, as well as their prior colleagues, including Andrew Crockett and Bill White. Helene Ray at the London Business School has been a fellow worrier about the consequences of the financial cycle, and I have learned a lot from her work.[2]

A book such as this one has many contributors. I thank Viral Acharya, Douglas Diamond, Yunzhi Hu, and Prachi Mishra, my longtime coauthors, for some of the work that underlies these chapters. Radhika Puri, my wife, reads and comments on everything I write and helps keep the arguments understandable. This is one of the many things for which I am forever indebted to her. I thank Thomas Jordan, president of the Swiss National Bank, for the invitation to give the 2019 Karl Brunner Lecture and Nicolas Cuche-Curti and Lukas Voellmy for helping me put together the book and reading through the drafts. Finally, I thank my editor, Laura Keeler, at the MIT Press.

1 A Step in the Dark: Unconventional Monetary Policy after the Crisis

In this chapter, based on a lightly edited and updated inaugural Andrew Crockett Memorial Lecture at the Bank for International Settlements (BIS) in June 2013, I lay out my concerns about the path monetary policy was taking in industrial countries after the Global Financial Crisis. Essentially, I argue that industrial countries were trying to solve a problem of unequal development within their countries with the wrong tools. As technological change undermined the economics of some sectors, regions, and professions, the right approach would have been to undertake structural reforms intended at elevating left-behind groups and communities and giving them the opportunity to participate fully in the changing economy. Instead, they focused on stimulus, largely through monetary means. The consequence, I worried, was ever-more aggressive monetary policy with potentially serious unintended consequences. Not least was the problem of how to dial back accommodative monetary policy when the economy had come to depend on it.

Sir Andrew Crockett was the general manager of the BIS between 1994 and 2003. In a speech he gave in 2001, entitled "Monetary Policy and Financial Stability," he argued that[1]

> the combination of a liberalised financial system and a fiat standard with monetary rules based exclusively in terms of inflation is not sufficient to secure financial stability. This is not to deny that inflation is often a source of financial instability. It certainly

is. . . . Yet the converse is not necessarily true. There are numerous examples of periods in which the restoration of price stability has provided fertile ground for excessive optimism.

He went on,

If an absence of inflation is not, by itself, sufficient to ensure financial stability . . . to what can we look to contain their build-up? The answer is, of course, prudential regulation. However, the tools of prudential regulation are themselves based on perceptions of risk which are not independent of the credit and asset price cycle. If prudential regulation depends on assessments of collateral, capital adequacy and so on, and if the valuation of assets is distorted, the bulwark against the build-up of financial imbalances will be weakened.

In these few paragraphs, Andrew Crockett summed up what has taken many of us an entire global financial crisis and years of research to learn. Using his lens, I want to go over the new tools of central banking, which come under the rubric "Unconventional Monetary Policies." Much of the time, I will be exploring the contours of what we don't know, asking questions rather than providing answers. But let us start at the beginning, to the deeper underlying causes of the recent financial and sovereign debt crisis in the United States and Europe. By its very nature, this discussion has to be speculative.

The Roots of the Crisis

Two competing narratives of the sources of the crisis and attendant remedies are emerging. The first and the better-known diagnosis is that demand has collapsed because of the high debt buildup prior to the crisis. The households (and countries) that were most prone to spend cannot borrow any more. To revive growth, others must be encouraged to spend—current account surplus countries should trim surpluses, governments that can still borrow should run larger deficits, and thrifty households should be dissuaded from saving through rock-bottom interest rates. Under these circumstances, budgetary recklessness is a virtue, at least in the short term. In the medium term, once growth revives, debt can be paid down and the financial sector curbed so that it does not inflict another crisis on the world.

But there is another narrative. And that is that the fundamental growth capacity in industrial countries has been shifting down for decades now, masked for a while by debt-fueled demand. More such demand, or asking for reckless spending from emerging markets, will not put us back on a sustainable path to growth. Instead, industrial democracies need to improve the environment for growth.

The first narrative is the standard Keynesian one, modified for a debt crisis. It is the one most government officials and central bankers, as well as Wall Street economists, subscribe to and needs little elaboration. The second narrative, in my view, offers a deeper and more persuasive view of the blight that afflicts our times. Let me flesh it out a bit.[2]

The 1950s and 1960s were a time of strong growth in the West and Japan. A number of factors, including rebuilding from wartime destruction; the resurgence of trade after the protectionist 1930s; the rolling out of new technologies in power, transport, and communications across countries; and the expansion in educational attainments all helped industrial countries grow. But as Tyler Cowen has argued in his book, *The Great Stagnation*, when these low-hanging fruits were plucked, it became much harder to propel growth from the 1970s onward.[3]

In the meantime, though, as Wolfgang Streeck wrote persuasively in a 2011 article in the *New Left Review*, when it

seemed like an eternity of innovation and growth stretched
ahead in the 1960s, democratic governments were quick to
pledge the fruits of future growth to their citizens in the form
of an expanded welfare state.[4] As growth subsequently faltered,
this meant government spending expanded, even while government resources shrank. For a while, central banks accommodated that spending. The resulting high levels of inflation
created widespread discontent, especially because little growth
resulted. Faith in Keynesian stimulus diminished, although
the high inflation did reduce public debt levels.

Central banks started focusing on low and stable inflation as their primary objective and increasingly became more
independent from their political masters. Government deficit spending, however, continued apace, and public debt as a
share of gross domestic product (GDP) in industrial countries
climbed steadily from the late 1970s, this time without the
benefit of unexpected inflation to reduce its real value.

Recognizing the need to find new sources of growth, the
United States toward the end of Jimmy Carter's term and then
under Ronald Reagan deregulated industry and the financial
sector, as did Margaret Thatcher's United Kingdom. Competition and innovation increased substantially in these countries.
Freer trade and the adoption of new technologies increased
the demand for, and incomes of, highly skilled, talented, and
educated workers doing nonroutine jobs like consulting. More
routine, once well-paying jobs done by the unskilled or the
moderately educated were automated or outsourced. So income
inequality emerged not primarily because of policies favoring
the rich but because the liberalized economy favored those
equipped to take advantage of it. A number of communities
within developed countries, especially those that depended on

a few large manufacturing employers that closed down, found themselves unable to take part in the new growth.

The shortsighted political response to the anxieties of those falling behind was to ease their access to credit. Faced with little regulatory and supervisory restraint, sometimes based on the faith that private incentives worked best in this best of all worlds, the financial system overdosed on risky mortgage and home equity loans to lower middle-class borrowers, aided and abetted by very low policy interest rates.

Continental Europe did not deregulate as much and preferred to seek growth in greater economic integration. But the price for protecting workers and firms was slower growth and higher unemployment. And, while inequality did not increase as much as in the United States, job prospects were terrible in the Euro periphery for the young and unemployed, who were left out of the protected system.

The advent of the euro was a seeming boon, because it reduced borrowing costs and allowed countries to create jobs through debt-financed spending. Unfortunately, spending pushed up wages, especially but not exclusively in the nontraded sectors like government and construction. Without a commensurate increase in productivity, the heavy spending countries became increasingly uncompetitive and indebted and started running large trade deficits.

Of course, it did not seem at that time that countries like Spain, with its low public debt and deficits, were overspending. But as Andrew Crockett foresaw, the boom masked lending problems as well as fiscal problems. Spanish government revenues were high on the back of the added activity and the additional taxes, and so spending seemed moderate. However, if spending was adjusted for the stage of the cycle, it was excessive.[5]

The important exception to this pattern was Germany, which was accustomed to low borrowing costs even before it entered the Eurozone. Germany had to contend with historically high unemployment, stemming from reunification with a sick East Germany. In the euro's initial years, Germany had no option but to reduce worker protections, limit wage increases, and reduce pensions as it tried to increase employment. Germany's labor costs fell relative to the rest of the Eurozone, and its exports and GDP growth exploded. Germany's exports, at least in part, were taken up by the spending Euro-periphery.

Eventually, the Global Financial Crisis (GFC) starting in 2007 brought debt-fueled spending to an end, whether by national governments (Greece), local governments (Spain), the construction sector (Ireland and Spain), or the financial sector (Ireland). The United States and Europe fell into recession, in part because debt-fueled demand disappeared but also because it had a multiplier effect on other sources of demand.

The Case for Unconventional Monetary Policies

The crisis was devastating in its impact. Entire markets collapsed, and depositors lost confidence in even the soundest banks and, over time, started losing faith in the debt of weak sovereigns. For the financial economist, perhaps the most vivid demonstration of the depth of the problems in the financial sector was that standard arbitrage relationships such as covered interest rate parity started breaking down.[6] There was money to be had without risk—provided one could borrow! And few could. The real economy was equally devastated. For a while, as economist Barry Eichengreen has pointed out, the downturn in economic activity tracked developments at the onset of the Great Depression.

Central banks prevented a second Great Depression. Hindsight is 20–20. It now seems obvious that central banks should have done what they did then, but in many ways, the central banks were making it up as they went. Fortunately for the world, much of what they did was exactly right. They eased access to liquidity through innovative programs such as the Troubled Assets Relief Program (TARP) in the United States or Long-Term Refinancing Operations (LTRO) in the Euro area. By lending long term without asking too many questions of the collateral they received, by buying assets beyond usual limits, and by focusing on repairing markets, they restored liquidity to a world financial system that would otherwise have been insolvent based on prevailing market asset prices. In this matter, central bankers are deservedly heroes in a world that has precious few of them.

If they are to be faulted at all on the rescue, perhaps it is that the repair the central bankers effected was too subtle for some. Conditional on the illiquid conditions, the financial system received an enormous fiscal subsidy—if central bank actions such as guarantees and purchases had not worked out, the taxpayer would have been hit with an enormous loss. But conditional on repairing the system, the subsidy seemed small. Not surprisingly, rescued bankers (and rescued countries) felt somewhat aggrieved when the rescuers expected them to change their behavior. Instead, the public saw large banker bonuses return, and banker attitudes implied the rescue was a great investment opportunity conferred on the rescuers. No wonder bankers unfortunately had a social status somewhere between that of a pimp and a conman after the GFC—as reflected in the abrupt fall in the number of our students in Chicago Booth's MBA program opting for careers as bankers. I say unfortunately, because more than ever, the world needs good banking to promote growth.

Be that as it may, the second stage of the rescue was to stimulate growth with ultra-low interest rates. And here the central banks have been far less successful. Let us try and understand why.

The Keynesian Explanation and an Alternative

According to the most influential Keynesian view, the root cause of continued high unemployment and a slow recovery is excessively high real interest rates. The logic is simple.[7] Before the financial crisis erupted in 2008, consumers buoyed US demand by borrowing heavily against their rising house prices. As the crisis hit, these heavily indebted households could not borrow and spend any more.

An important source of aggregate demand evaporated. As indebted consumers stopped buying, real (inflation-adjusted) interest rates should have fallen to encourage hitherto thrifty debt-free households to spend. But real interest rates did not fall enough, because nominal interest rates cannot be reduced below zero—the so-called zero lower bound became a constraint on growth.[8]

The Keynesian explanation suggests that the full-employment equilibrium real interest rate in the postcrisis overleveraged world—the so-called neutral rate—should be strongly negative. This has been the justification for central banks to employ innovative policies to try and achieve ultra-low real interest rates. That the low rates do not seem to have enhanced growth rates quickly has only made central bankers even more innovative.

But what if low interest rates do not enhance demand in a postcrisis world beyond a point? While low rates may encourage spending if credit were easy to obtain, it is not at all clear that corporations or traditional savers today will go out and spend. Think of the soon-to-retire office worker. She saved because she wanted enough money to retire. Given the terrible returns on savings since 2007, the prospect of continuing low interest rates might make her put even more money aside. Indeed, in simple models of the kind that the Keynesians propose, the existence of savers who have suffered a loss of savings and have end-of-working-life savings objectives can imply that lower real interest rates are contractionary—savers put more money aside as interest rates fall in order to meet the savings they think they will need when they retire.[9]

The point is not that this is a strong argument that ultra-low interest rates will have a net perverse effect but that a crisis potentially creates offsetting effects even on aggregate demand (through a readjustment of savings plans) that make it difficult to argue, based on theory, that strongly negative real interest rates are the right medicine to restore demand. Years of strongly negative real interest rates might contribute only weakly to demand growth.

There are two further problems in the view that a restoration of undifferentiated aggregate demand is the right solution. First, after a debt-fueled boom, the paucity of demand is localized in certain social classes, certain regions, and certain productive sectors. Second, in the years leading up to a debt crisis, it is not only demand that is distorted through borrowing but also supply.

To see all this, let us focus for the moment on household borrowing. Before the crisis in the United States, when borrowing became easier, it was not the well-to-do, whose spending is not constrained by their incomes, who increased their consumption; rather, the increase came from poorer and younger families whose needs and dreams far outpaced their incomes.[10] Their needs can be different from those of the rich.

Moreover, the goods that were easiest to buy were those that were easiest to post as collateral—houses and cars, rather than perishables. And rising house prices in some regions made it easier to borrow more to spend on other daily needs such as diapers and baby food.

The point is that debt-fueled demand emanated from particular households in particular regions for particular goods. While it catalyzed a more generalized demand—the elderly plumber who worked longer hours in the boom spent more on his stamp collection—it was not unreasonable to believe that much of debt-fueled demand was more focused. So, as lending dried up, borrowing households could no longer spend, and demand for certain goods changed disproportionately, especially in areas that boomed earlier.

Of course, the effects spread through the economy—as demand for cars fell, the demand for steel also fell, and steel workers were laid off. But as my colleague Amir Sufi and his coauthor, Atif Mian, have shown, unemployment, household overindebtedness, and the consequent fall in demand were localized in specific regions where house prices rose particularly rapidly.[11] Hairdressers in Las Vegas lost their jobs because households there skipped on expensive hairdos when they were left with too much debt stemming from the housing bust. Even if ultra-low real interest rates coerce older debt-free savers to spend more, it is unlikely that there are enough of them in Las Vegas or that they want the hairdos that younger house buyers desired. And if these debt-free savers are in New York City, which did not experience as much of a boom and a bust, cutting real interest rates will encourage spending on haircuts in New York City, which already has plenty of demand, but not in Las Vegas, which has too little.[12]

Similarly, one could argue that even healthy firms do not invest in the bust, not because they face a high cost of capital but because there is uncertainty about where, when, and how demand will reappear. In sum, the bust that follows years of a debt-fueled boom leaves behind an economy that supplies too much of the wrong kind of goods or services relative to the changed demand. Unlike a normal cyclical recession, in which demand falls across the board and recovery requires merely rehiring laid-off workers to resume their old jobs, economic recovery following a lending bust typically requires workers to move across industries and to new locations because the old debt-fueled demand varied both across sectors and geographically and cannot be revived quickly.[13]

There is thus a subtle but important difference between the debt-driven demand view and the Keynesian explanation that deleveraging (saving by chastened borrowers) or debt overhang (the inability of debt-laden borrowers to spend) is responsible for slow postcrisis growth. Both views accept that the central source of weak aggregate demand is the disappearance of demand from former borrowers. But they differ on solutions.

The Keynesian wants to boost demand generally. They believe that all demand is equal. But if we believe that debt-driven demand is different, the demand stimulated by ultra-low interest rates will at best be palliative. There is both a humanitarian and an economic case for writing down the debt of borrowers when they have little hope of paying it back.[14] Writing down former borrowers' debt may even be effective in producing the old pattern of demand. But relying on the formerly indebted to borrow and spend so that the old economy reemerges is irresponsible. And different new borrowers may want to spend on different things, so fueling a new credit boom may be an ineffective (and unsustainable) way to get full employment back.[15]

If the differentiated demand that emerged in the boom is hard or irresponsible to re-create, the sustainable solution is to allow the supply side to adjust to more normal and sustainable sources of demand. Some of that adjustment is a matter of time as individuals adjust to changed circumstances. And some requires relative price adjustments and structural reforms that will generate sustainable growth—for example, allowing wages to adjust and creating ways for bankers, construction workers, and autoworkers to retrain for faster-growing industries. But relative price adjustments and structural reforms take time to produce results.

In the meantime, we have had plenty of stimulus. The political compulsions that abetted the boom also mandated urgency in the bust. Industrial countries that relied on borrowing to speed up growth typically wanted faster results. With the room for fiscal stimulus limited, monetary policy became the tool of choice to restore growth. And the Keynesian argument—that the equilibrium or neutral real interest rate is ultra-low—has become the justification for more and more monetary innovation.

Unconventional Monetary Policies Focused on Ultra-Low Rates

I have argued that unconventional central bank policies to repair markets and fix institutions worked. Even the European Central Bank's promise to do what it takes through the Outright Monetary Transaction (OMT) program to bolster sovereign debt has bought sovereigns time to undertake reforms, although a fair debate could be had on whether this implicit guarantee has a quasi-fiscal element.[16] As we have seen earlier, it is the central bank's willingness to accept significant losses contingent on its intervention being ineffective that allows it to move the market to a new trading equilibrium where it does not suffer losses. Many interventions to infuse liquidity have an implicit fiscal element to them, and OMT is no exception.

Let us turn now to unconventional monetary policy intended to force the real interest rate very low.[17] As I have argued above, the view that the full-employment equilibrium real interest rate is strongly negative can be questioned. Once that is in doubt, the whole program of pushing rates lower as a way of moving the economy back to full employment is also questionable. But I want to move on to focus here on the zero lower-bound problem. I will then turn to whether low rates are being transmitted into activity.

Which interest rate is the operative one for influencing economic activity? Clearly, the long-term rate matters for discounting asset prices such as stocks and bonds, as well as long-term fixed asset investment, while the short-term rate affects the cost of capital for entities engaged in maturity transformation. The interest rate channel (where the central bank affects consumption, savings, and investment decisions through the interest rate), the asset price channel (where the central bank aims to alter asset prices and thus household wealth and risk tolerance through interest rates), the credit channel (where the central bank affects the valuation of firm and bank balance sheets and thereby alters the volume of credit), and the exchange rate channel (whereby the central bank affects the exchange rate) all probably work through a combination of short and long rates with varying degrees of emphasis on each part of the term structure.[18]

The central bank directly controls the policy rate and thus the short-term nominal rate. The zero lower-bound problem stems from its inability to push the short-term nominal policy interest rate below zero. Further reductions in the short-term real rate will come only if it can push up inflationary expectations.

Because long-term nominal interest rates are typically above zero even when the policy rate is zero, the central bank can try to push down long-term nominal rates directly. Of course, an immediate question is why the long-term nominal rate stays above zero when the equilibrium long rate is lower. One possible answer is that arbitrage from rolling over short investment strategies using the higher-than-equilibrium expected short rate holds the long rate higher than it should be.

So two strategies of bringing down the nominal long rate present themselves: first, commit to holding the short rate at zero over time even beyond the point when normalizing it would be in order. This is what the Fed calls *forward guidance*. Second, buy long-term bonds, thus creating more appetite for the remaining ones in public hands, thus pushing down the long rate. The Fed aims to use its large-scale asset purchase (LSAP) program to take long bonds out of private portfolios with the hope that as they *rebalance their portfolios*, the price of long bonds (and other assets) will rise and yields will fall.[19] The Bank of Japan wants to add to these strategies by raising inflationary expectations, which is not an explicit objective of the Fed.[20] Neither central bank talks about depreciating the exchange rate as a central objective, although they do not rule it out as a side effect.

One could ask whether these policies should work even theoretically. Forward guidance relies on the central bank being willing to hold down policy rates way into the future below what would otherwise be appropriate—below, for example, that suggested by the Taylor Rule.[21] Thus, it implicitly implies a willingness to tolerate higher inflation levels in the future. But what ensures such commitment? Will the fear of breaking a prior transparent explicit promise (say to hold policy rates at zero so long as unemployment is above 6.5 percent, inflation is below 2.5 percent, and long-term inflationary expectations are well anchored) weigh heavily on the governors? Or will they fudge their way out when the time comes by saying that long-term expectations have become less well anchored?

Some argue that the source of commitment will be the LSAP itself. The central bank may fear losing value on its bond holdings if it raises rates too early. However, one could equally well argue that it could fear a rise in inflationary expectations if it stays on hold too long, which in turn could decimate the value of its bond holdings.

It may well be that LSAPs are really a signaling device for forward guidance—the central bank is essentially telling the markets that so long as LSAPs are under way, it will not raise rates. So the normalization of interest rates will happen only after a well-advertised and sufficiently drawn-out end to the asset purchase program.[22]

And then we have the asset purchase program itself. If markets are not segmented, a version of the Modigliani–Miller theorem or Ricardian equivalence suggests that the Fed cannot alter interest rates by buying bonds. Essentially, the representative agent will see through the Fed's purchases. Since the aggregate portfolio that has to be held by the economy does not change, pricing will not change. Alternatively, households will undo what the Fed does.[23] For LSAPs to work, the market must be segmented with some agents being nonparticipants in some markets. Alternatively, the market must not internalize the Fed's portfolio holdings. As with forward guidance, this argument for the effectiveness of LSAPs makes it an empirical question.

Much of the evidence on the effectiveness of asset purchase programs comes from the first Fed LSAP, which involved buying agency and mortgage-backed securities in the midst of the crisis. Fed purchases restored some confidence to those markets (including by signaling that the government stood behind agency debt), and this had large effects on the yields. Event studies document that the effects on yields in the following rounds of LSAPs were much smaller.[24]

Regardless of the effect Fed purchases may have had on the way in, speculation in May 2013 that it would start tapering its asset purchases led to significant increases in Treasury yields and large adverse effects on the prices of risky assets and cross-border capital flows. This is surprising given the theory, because what matters to the portfolio balance argument is the stock of long-term assets in the Fed's portfolio, not the flow. So long as the Fed can be trusted to hold on to the stock, the price of risky assets should hold up. Yet the market seems to have reacted to news about the possible tapering of Fed flows into the market, which one would have thought would have small effect on the expected stock. Either the market concluded that Fed implicit promises about holding on to the stock of assets it had bought were not credible, or it expected LSAPs to continue for much longer before it was disabused (which also brought forward the eventual normalization of interest rates), or we do not understand as much about how LSAPs work as we should!

Given that long-term nominal bond yields in Japan are already low, the Bank of Japan's focus has been more directly on enhancing inflationary expectations than on pushing down nominal yields. One of the benefits of the enormous firepower that a central bank can bring to bear is the ability to unsettle entrenched expectations. The shock and awe generated by the Bank of Japan's quantitative and qualitative easing program may have been what was needed to dislodge entrenched deflationary expectations.

The Bank of Japan hopes that direct monetary financing of the large fiscal deficit will raise inflationary expectations. A collateral benefit as the currency depreciates is inflation imported through exchange rate depreciation. Nevertheless, the Bank of Japan's task is not easy. If it is too successful in raising inflationary expectations, nominal bond yields will rise rapidly and bond prices will tank. So to avoid roiling bond investors, it has to raise inflationary expectations just enough to bring the long-term real rate down to what is consistent with equilibrium *without altering nominal bond yields too much*. And given that we really do not know what the neutral or equilibrium real rate is, how much inflationary expectation to generate is a matter of guesswork.

The bottom line is that unconventional monetary policies that move away from repairing markets or institutions to changing prices and inflationary expectations seem to be a step into the dark. Of course, central bankers could argue that their bread-and-butter business is to change asset prices and alter inflationary expectations by changing the policy rate. However, unconventional policies are assumed to work through different channels. We cannot be sure of their value, even leaving aside the theoretical questions I raised earlier about pushing down the real rate to ultra-low levels as a way to full employment. Let us now turn to their unintended side effects.

The Unintended Effects of Unconventional Policies

Risk Taking and Investment Distortions

If effective, the combination of the "low for long" policy for short-term policy rates, coupled with quantitative easing, tends to depress yields across the yield curve for fixed-income securi-ties. Institutional fixed-income investors with some nominal return needs (for instance, pension funds that have promised fixed nominal payments to pensioners) then migrate to riskier instruments such as junk bonds, emerging market bonds, or commodity exchange-traded funds. Other investors migrate to stocks. To some extent, this reach for yield is precisely one of the intended consequences of unconventional monetary policy. The hope is that as the price of risk is reduced, cor-porations faced with a lower cost of capital will have greater incentive to make real investments, thereby creating jobs and enhancing growth.

There are two ways these calculations can go wrong. First, financial risk taking may stay just that, without translating into real investment. For instance, the price of junk debt or existing homes may be bid up unduly, increasing the risk of a crash, without new capital goods being bought or homes being built. This is especially likely if key supports to invest-ment such as a functioning and well-capitalized banking sys-tem, zoning permissions for new housing, or policy certainty are missing. A number of authors point out the financial risk-taking incentives engendered by very accommodative or unconventional monetary policy, with Stein (2013) pro-viding a comprehensive view of the associated economic downsides.[25] As just one example, the IMF's Global Financial Stability Report (Spring 2013) points to the reemergence of covenant-lite loans as evidence that greater risk tolerance may be morphing into risk insouciance.

Second, and probably a lesser worry, accommodative policies may reduce the cost of capital for firms so much that they prefer labor-saving capital investment to hiring labor. The falling share of labor in recent years is consistent with a low cost of capital, although there are other explanations. Excessive labor-saving capital investment may defeat the very purpose of unconventional policies, that is, greater employment. Relatedly, by changing asset prices and distorting price signals, unconventional monetary policy may cause overinvestment in areas where asset prices or credit are particularly sensitive to low interest rates. For instance, the economy may get too many buildings and too few machines, a consequence that is all too recent to forget.

Spillovers—Capital Flows and Exchange Rate Appreciation and Credit Booms

The spillovers from easy global liquidity conditions to cross-border gross banking flows, exchange rate appreciation, stock market appreciation, and asset price and credit booms in capital receiving countries—and eventual overextension, current account deficits, and asset price busts—have been documented elsewhere, both for precrisis Europe and postcrisis emerging markets.[26] The transmission mechanism appears to be that easy availability of borrowing increases asset prices, increases bank capitalization, reduces perceived leverage, and reduces risk perceptions and measures (as indicated by the VIX index or value at risk), all of which feed back into more credit and actual leverage.[27] When this occurs cross-border, exchange rate appreciation in the receiving country is an additional factor that makes lending appear safer (I will elaborate on this mechanism in chapter 2). The concerns Andrew Crockett laid out have been observed repeatedly.[28]

For the receiving country, it is unclear whether monetary policy should be tightened at the risk of attracting more inflows or be accommodative and fuel the credit boom. Tighter fiscal policy is a textbook solution to contain aggregate demand, but it is politically difficult to tighten when revenues are booming, for the boom masks weakness, and the lack of obvious problems makes countermeasures politically difficult. Put differently, as I will argue later, industrial country central bankers justify unconventional policies because politicians are not taking the necessary decisions in their own countries—unconventional policies are the only game in town. At the same time, however, they expect receiving countries to follow textbook reactions to capital inflows, without acknowledging that these too may be politically difficult. The new received wisdom is to implement prudential measures, including capital controls, to contain credit expansion, but their effectiveness against a "wall of capital inflows" has yet to be established. Spain's countercyclical provisioning norms prior to the Global Financial Crisis may have prevented worse outcomes but could not prevent the damage that the credit and construction boom did to Spain.

Even if the unconventional monetary policies that focus on lowering interest rates across the term structure have limited effects on interest rates in the large, liquid, sending-country Treasury markets, the volume of flows they generate could swamp the more illiquid receiving-country markets, thus creating large price and volume effects. The reality may be that the wall of capital dispatched by sending countries may far outweigh the puny defenses that most receiving countries have to offset its effects. What may work theoretically may not be of the right magnitude in practice to offset procyclical effects and, even if it is of the right magnitude, may not be politically feasible. As leverage in the receiving country builds up, vulnerabilities mount, and these are quickly exposed when markets sense an end to the unconventional policies and reverse the flows.

The important concern during the Great Depression was competitive devaluation. While receiving countries have complained about "currency wars" in the recent past, and both China and South Korea seem affected by the sizable Japanese depreciation after the Bank of Japan embarked on quantitative and qualitative easing (though they benefited earlier when the yen was appreciating), the more worrisome effect of unconventional monetary policies may well be *competitive asset price inflation*.

We have seen credit and asset price inflation circle around the globe. While industrial countries suffered from excessive credit expansion as their central banks accommodated the global savings glut after the dot-com bust, emerging markets have been the recipients of search-for-yield flows following the global financial crisis. This time around, because of the collapse of export markets, they have been far more willing to follow accommodative policies themselves, as a result of which they have experienced credit and asset price booms. Countries like Brazil and India that were close to external balance have started running large current account deficits. Unsustainable demand has traveled full circle, back to emerging markets, and emerging markets are being forced to adjust. Will they be able to put their house in order in time? (As I wrote this, the taper tantrum, set off by then Chairman Bernanke's speech in May 2013 that the Federal Reserve would have to start tapering quantitative easing, started engulfing these countries, with significant amounts of capital flowing out in a short period of time.)

What should be done? How do we prevent the monetary reaction to asset price busts from becoming the genesis of asset price booms elsewhere? In a world integrated by massive capital flows, monetary policy in large countries serves as a common accelerator pedal for the globe. One's car might languish in a deep ditch even when the accelerator pedal is pressed fully down, but the rest of the world might be pushed way beyond the speed limit. If there is little way for countries across the globe to avoid the spillovers from unconventional policies emanating from the large central banks, should the large central banks internalize these spillovers?[29] How? And will it be politically feasible? This is something we will come back to in chapter 3.

Postponing Reform and Moral Hazard

Central bankers do get aggrieved when questioned about their uncharacteristic role as innovators. "What would you have us do when we are the only game in town?" they ask. But that may well be the problem. When central bankers offer themselves as the only game in town, in an environment where politicians only have choices between the bad and the worse, they become the only game in town. Everyone cedes the stage to the central banker, who cannot admit that their tools are untried and of unknown efficacy. Central bankers have to be seen as confident and will constantly refer to the many bullets they still have even if they have very few. But that very public confidence traps them because the public wants to know why they are not doing more.

The dilemma for central bankers is particularly acute when the immediate prospect of a terrible economic crisis is necessary for politicians to obtain the room to do the unpleasant but right thing. For instance, repeated crises forced politicians in the euro area to the bargaining table as they accepted what was domestically unpopular, for they could sell it to their constituents as necessary to avert the worse outcome of an immediate euro breakup. The jury is still out on whether the Outright Monetary Transactions (OMT) program announced by the European Central Bank, essentially as a fulfillment of the pledge to do what it takes to protect and preserve the euro, bought the time necessary for politicians to undertake difficult institutional reform or whether it allowed narrow domestic concerns to take center stage again.

And finally, there is the issue of moral hazard. Clearly, when the system is about to collapse, it is hard to argue that it should be allowed to collapse to teach posterity a lesson. Not only can the loss of institutional capital be very hard for the economy to rebuild, but the cost of the collapse may ensure that no future central banker ever contemplates "disciplining" the system. And clearly, few central bankers would like to be known for allowing the collapse on their watch. But equally clearly, the knowledge that the central bank will intervene in tail outcomes gives private bankers an incentive to ignore such outcomes and hold too little liquidity or move with the herd.[30] All this is well known now. Less clear is what to do about it, especially because it is still not obvious whether bankers flirt with tail risks because they expect to be bailed out or because they are ignorant of the risks.[31] Concerns about moral hazard are, of course, irrelevant if bankers are merely ignorant! Once again, we do not know.

Exit

Having experienced the side effects of unconventional monetary policies on "entry," many now worry about exit from those policies. The problem is that while "entry" may take a long time as the central bank needs to build credibility about its future policies to have effect, "exit" may not require central bank credibility and may be anticipated, with its consequences brought forward by the market. Asset prices are unlikely to remain stable if the key intent of entry was to move asset prices from equilibrium. What was lifted up unnaturally must fall, unless our economies have been transported to an entirely new environment, which is unlikely.

One might think that countries that have complained about unconventional monetary policies in industrial countries should be happy with exit. The key complication is leverage. If asset prices simply went up and down, the withdrawal of unconventional policies should restore status quo ante. However, leverage built up in sectors with hitherto rising asset prices can bring down firms, financiers, and even whole economies when asset prices fall.[32] There is no use saying that everyone should have anticipated the consequences of the end of unconventional policies. As Andrew Crockett put it in his speech, "Financial intermediaries are better at assessing relative risks at a point in time, than projecting the evolution of risk over the financial cycle."

Countries around the world have to prepare themselves, especially with adequate supplies of liquidity. Exiting central bankers have to be prepared to "enter" again if the consequences of exit are too abrupt. Will exit occur smoothly, in fits and starts, or abruptly? This is yet another aspect of unconventional monetary policies that we know little about.

Conclusion

Churchill could well have said on the subject of unconventional monetary policy, "Never in the field of economic policy has so much been spent, with so little evidence, by so few." Unconventional monetary policy has truly been a step in the dark. But this does raise the question of why central bankers have departed from their usual conservatism—after all, "innovative" is usually an epithet for a central banker.

A view from emerging markets is that, in the past, crises have typically occurred in countries that did not have the depth of economic thinking that the United States or Europe has. When emerging market policymakers were faced with orthodox economic advice that suggested many years of austerity and unemployment as well as widespread bank closures were needed to cleanse the economy after a crisis, they did not protest. After all, few had the training and confidence to question the orthodoxy, and the ones that nevertheless did so were considered misguided cranks. Multilateral institutions, empowered by their control over funding, dictated policy from the economic scriptures.

When the crisis did hit at home, however, Western-based economists were much less willing to accept that pain was necessary. The Fed, led by perhaps the foremost monetary economist in the world, proposed creative solutions that few in policy circles, including the usually conservative multilateral institutions, questioned. After all, they no longer had the influence of the purse or the advantage in economic training. So the explanation for the abandonment of orthodoxy is that top economists reexamined their remedies when the painful adjustment had to be undertaken at home.

This is, however, not a satisfactory explanation. After all, Nobel laureates like Joe Stiglitz, whatever one may think about his remedies, did protest very publicly about the adjustment programs the multilateral institutions were imposing on the Asian economies.

Consider another explanation—perhaps the success that central bankers had in preventing the collapse of the financial system after the GFC secured them the public's trust to go further into the deeper waters of quantitative easing. Could success at rescuing the banks have also misled some central bankers into thinking they had the Midas touch? So a combination of public confidence, tinged with central banker hubris, could explain the foray into quantitative easing. Yet this too seems only a partial explanation. For few among the lay public were happy that the bankers were rescued, and many on Main Street did not understand why the financial system had to be saved when their own employers were laying off workers or closing down.

Let me try again. Perhaps it was the political difficulty of doing nothing after spending billions rescuing the private bankers that encouraged central bankers to act creatively. After all, how could one let a technical hitch like the zero lower bound (ZLB) come in the way of rescuing Main Street when innovative facilities such as TARP had been used to save Wall Street? Was it that once central bankers undertook the necessary rescues of banks, they were irremediably entangled in politics, and quantitative easing was an inevitable outcome?

Or perhaps it was simply common decency: being in a position of responsibility, and in a world where much had broken down, central bankers decided to do whatever they could, which included instruments like quantitative easing.

As with much about recent unconventional monetary policies, there is a lot we can only guess at. The bottom line is that
if there is one myth that recent developments have exploded,
it is probably the one that sees central bankers as technocrats,
hovering cleanly over the politics and ideologies of their
time. Their feet too have touched the ground.

On a more practical note, let me end with a caution from
Andrew Crockett's speech:

> The costs of uncontrolled financial cycles are sufficiently large that
> avenues for resisting them should at least be explored. At a mini-
> mum, it seems reasonable to suggest that, in formulating monetary
> policy aimed at an inflation objective, central banks should take
> explicit account of the impact of financial developments on the
> balance of risks.

Then as now, this is very good advice.

2 Capital Flows, Liquidity, and Leverage: A New Take on Monetary Policy Spillovers

Before the Global Financial Crisis, there was a sense among policy-makers that the world had arrived at a policy optimum, which had contributed to a "great moderation" in economic volatility. In this world, the sole objective for monetary policy was domestic price stability, and it was achieved by flexible inflation targeting. By allowing the exchange rate to respond as needed, the system eliminated the need for exchange rate intervention or reserve accumulation. Inflation targeting plus floating exchange rates, as Eichengreen et al. (2011) argued, "could thus be regarded as the triumph of the 'own house in order' doctrine in the international monetary field. National macroeconomic stability was seen as sufficient for international macroeconomic stability. The domestic and international aspects were essentially regarded as two sides of the same coin."

A vast body of research since the Global Financial Crisis of 2007–2009 suggests this view is too complacent. There are large policy spillovers between countries that cannot be offset by adopting standard nostrums such as allowing exchange rates to adjust. Specifically, easy monetary policy in source funding currencies appears to be transmitted to receiving countries via capital flows, receiving-country currency appreciation, a rise in borrowing, and an increase in prices of financial and real assets there. These lead to financial fragility. However, these findings raise important questions. If borrowing and lending are rational, why do market participants lever up knowing the associated risks? Why do financing conditions change so suddenly—is this about fundamentals? What can country authorities do to reduce the associated systemic risks? This is the subject of chapter 2, which was delivered as the Karl Brunner Lecture at the Swiss National Bank.

Cross-border capital flows are neither an unmitigated blessing nor an undoubted curse. Used judiciously, they can be beneficial to recipient countries, making up deficiencies in the availability of long-term risk capital and reducing gaps in local corporate governance. They can also be beneficial to sending countries, offering investment avenues for savings generated by aging populations.

Of course, capital flows can also be problematic. They can come at the wrong time, adding further credit to a raging investment boom and fueling asset-price bubbles. They can come in the wrong form—held as short-term claims on corporations or the government, with the option to leave at a moment's notice. And they can leave at the wrong time, when the lure of higher interest rates in sending countries summons them back, instead of when projects in the receiving countries are completed. As with dynamite, whether cross-border capital flows are good or bad depends on how they are used. Unfortunately, there are no obvious policy remedies to tame capital inflows and to rearrange their timing to the benefit of recipient countries. Even if there were, receiving-country institutions are often not up to the task—easy money is hard to turn down for even the most sensible policymakers.

Recipient countries are, of course, not the only relevant players. A particularly important factor in "pushing" and "pulling" cross-border capital flows is the stance of monetary policy in advanced economies. Easy monetary policy is transmitted to receiving countries via capital flows, currency appreciation, a rise in borrowing, and an increase in prices of financial and real assets. All this is reversed when monetary policy tightens, albeit with a critical difference. The buildup of receiving-country corporate and government borrowing in the easing phase leads to financial fragility during the tightening phase.

What can emerging-market economies do to reduce the risks associated with large, sustained capital flows, especially in the face of "low for long" monetary policies in advanced countries that we discussed in the previous chapter? What responsibility should central banks in advanced economies bear for the impact of their monetary policies abroad, and what steps can they take to limit the impact? Is there a role for international financial institutions such as the IMF?

The Model: The Domestic Corporate Side

To shed further light on these issues, I describe a model of domestic corporate financing based on work with Douglas Diamond and Yunzhi Hu, which I will subsequently use to discuss the effects of monetary policy, capital flows, and exchange rates on the corporate sector.[1] The key element in the model is that sustained expectations of high future liquidity (in the sense that potential asset buyers are wealthy and can pay high prices for corporate assets) can incentivize the corporate sector to lever up. The combination of high leverage and high expected liquidity reduces corporate incentives to maintain high levels of corporate governance or pledgeability. The fall-off in governance is not a problem when high liquidity is sustained but does become problematic when liquidity dries up, since there is then very little supporting the ability of corporations to roll over their debt or borrow anew. Put differently, high expectations of liquidity create the conditions where corporations become dependent on future liquidity to roll over their debt. When it does not materialize, they experience a sudden stop. Note that this can occur even if economic prospects for corporations are still bright. I will then argue that monetary policy-induced capital flows and their exchange rate effects are a quasi-exogenous source of fluctuations in a country's corporate sector's liquidity conditions and asset prices and are a source therefore of fluctuations in leverage and financial fragility.

Let us be more specific about the domestic corporate financing model, after which I will explain the role of source country monetary policy, capital flows, and exchange rates. Consider an economy where expert managers are needed to produce cash flow from assets we call firms. A number of existing firms are initially up for auction to the experts (this is a modeling convenience to establish initial debt levels for the firms). We will call the successful bidder in each firm the incumbent. The unsuccessful bidders bide their time, hoping to buy firms in the future from incumbents. Financiers, who don't really know how to run firms but have funds, are the other agents in the model.

Experts bid for the firm in the initial auction using both their initial wealth and anything they can borrow from financiers against the firm's assets. Financiers lend knowing they have two sorts of control rights to enforce repayment: first, control through the right to repossess and sell the firm if payments are missed and, second, control over the disposition of cash flows generated by the firm. The first right only requires the frictionless enforcement of property rights in the economy, which we assume. It has especial value when there are a large number of outside expert buyers willing to pay a high price for the firm's assets in the future—to get repayment, a lender can simply seize the firm and sell it to the highest bidder. Greater future wealth among outside experts (which we term *liquidity*) increases the availability of this *asset-sale-based* financing to a bidder in the initial auction.

The second type of control right is conferred on creditors by the firm's incumbent manager as they make the firm's cash flows more appropriable by, or pledgeable to, creditors over the medium term—for example, by improving accounting quality or setting up escrow accounts so that cash flows are hard to divert. We assume enhancing pledgeability takes time to set up but is also semi-durable (improving accounting quality is not instantaneous because it requires adopting new systems and hiring reputable people). So the incumbent manager sets pledgeability one period in advance, and it lasts a period. Pledgeability therefore stands for ways the firm's management can improve (or neglect) corporate governance. Importantly, it will increase the ability of anyone who owns the firm next period to borrow against its cash flows since those cash flows will be more pledgeable to lenders.

In general, both higher prospective wealth for experts (that is, liquidity) and the higher ability of an expert to borrow against the future cash flow of the firm they buy (that is, pledgeability) will increase their bids for the firm at a future date. Higher prospective bids will increase debt recovery by any creditor then and thus the willingness of creditors to lend upfront. So *higher future liquidity and pledgeability increase the ability of bidders in the initial auction to augment their bids with borrowing.*

However, pledgeability is determined by the incumbent firm manager after successfully buying the firm and taking on debt. What goes into this decision? The incumbent wants the future market valuation for the firm to be high—given the possibility they may have to sell the firm entirely if they have some need for money or sell a claim on it if they want to finance additional investment. So they have some personal incentive to raise pledgeability after buying the firm so that future bids for the firm are high. However, because they have taken on debt to finance their initial bid, enhancing *cash flow pledgeability* is a double-edged sword. The higher future bid from experts also enables existing creditors to collect more if the incumbent stays in control because the creditors have the right to seize assets and sell them to experts for more when not paid in full. In such situations, the incumbent has to "buy" the firm from creditors, by outbidding experts (or paying debt fully). *The higher the outstanding debt taken on initially, the lower the incumbent's incentive to raise pledgeability.* In contrast, the higher the probability the incumbent has to sell the firm or to raise new finance, the higher her incentive to raise pledgeability.

Now consider the effect of future liquidity on pledgeability choice. If experts are rational, they will never pay more for the firm in the future than its fundamental value. When future liquidity turns out to be very high, experts will have enough wealth to buy the firm at full value without needing to borrow more against the firm's future cash flows. If so, higher pledgeability has no effect on how much experts will bid to pay for the firm. In other words, *high future liquidity crowds out the need for pledgeability* in enhancing debt repayments. Therefore, we have two influences on pledgeability—the level of outstanding debt and the anticipated liquidity of experts. Now consider the interaction between the two.

Suppose an economic boom, where experts will have plenty of wealth, is thought very likely to occur. Repayment of any initial corporate borrowing is enforced by the potential high resale value of the firm—at the future date, wealthy experts will bid full value for the firm without needing high pledgeability to make their bid. The high anticipated resale value increases the promised payment that a firm can credibly repay and thus the amount any expert can borrow upfront to bid for the firm.

Since pledgeability is not needed to enforce repayment in a future highly liquid state, a high probability of such a state encourages creditors to lend large amounts upfront to the incumbent, even though they know high levels of debt crowd out the incumbent's incentive to enhance pledgeability. Furthermore, they will lend even if there is a possible low liquidity state where pledgeability is needed to enhance expert bids and thus creditor rights. *Prospective liquidity encourages high borrowing, which can crowd out pledgeability.* Subsequently, if the low liquidity state is realized, the enforceability of the firm's debt, as well as its borrowing capacity, will fall significantly because pledgeability has been set low. Experts, also hit by the downturn, no longer have much personal wealth, nor does the low cash flow pledgeability of the firm allow them to borrow against future cash flows to pay for acquiring the firm. Given outside bids for the firm are low, creditors' ability to enforce debt repayment falls. Refinancing dries up, and credit spreads rise substantially. They will stay high until the firm raises pledgeability, which will take time, or until liquidity rises again in the economy, which could take even longer.

An analogy from housing booms helps explain the dynamic. If a mortgage lender knows a house can easily be repossessed and sold profitably because houses are selling like hot cakes for high prices, what need is there to investigate the mortgage applicant further to determine whether they have a job or income? Normal safeguards and due diligence on loans are dispensed with in times of high prospective liquidity. One result during the US housing bubble was the infamous Ninja loan extended to borrowers with no income, no job, and no assets. Our point is that an individual firm's experience in a domestic credit boom provides a useful parallel. Sustained expectations of high future liquidity (in the sense that potential asset buyers are wealthy and can pay high prices for corporate assets) can incentivize companies to load up on debt; from the borrower's side, debt financing is always welcome because it allows the borrower to run an enterprise with less of its own money at stake. From the lender's side, high anticipated liquidity makes it easier to recover debt—if the borrower fails to pay, the lender can seize the firm's assets through a chapter 11 bankruptcy and sell them to someone else at a high price. The combination of high leverage and high expected liquidity, however, also reduces managerial incentives to put in place structures to constrain managerial misbehavior. The reason: if financing is expected to be plentiful, why put in place costly and constraining structures (such as good accounting rules, financial covenants, and an unimpeachable auditor) when much more additional financing is unlikely to be needed?

So far, so domestic. Let me summarize the ingredients. There is upfront competition for assets, and experts with limited wealth borrow as much as possible (against the firm's assets) to bid enough to be successful. Lenders depend on high future bids by other outside experts to enforce debt claims. These bids are enhanced by both higher cash flow pledgeability (set by the incumbent after buying the firm) and the liquidity (that is, wealth) of possible future bidders. A sharp increase in anticipated liquidity both enhances upfront borrowing, as well as depresses the pledgeability the incumbent sets. The deterioration in governance is not a problem when high liquidity is sustained, but it does become problematic when liquidity dries up, since there is then very little supporting the ability of corporations to borrow. Put differently, high expectations of liquidity create the conditions where corporations become dependent on continued future liquidity to roll over their debt. When it does not materialize, they experience a sudden stop. This can occur even if economic prospects for corporations are still bright.

The Model: The International Side

Let us now situate this firm in an emerging market (or a peripheral European country). We add three more assumptions based on the vast emerging evidence. First, domestic companies in the emerging market (the experts in the model) have a substantial amount of outstanding borrowing from countries that are the source of capital outflows or denominated in the currency of those countries even if sourced elsewhere. The source country is typically the United States and the currency the dollar, although our point is more general (see, for example, Gopinath and Stein [2021] for why domestic companies may take on foreign currency debt).

Second, easier (tighter) monetary policy in the source country gets transmitted into domestic currency appreciation (depreciation) in the capital-receiving emerging market.[2] Since "experts," the domestic firms in the emerging market, already have foreign currency borrowing, this means their net worth, and hence their liquidity, will be anticipated to increase as the amount of domestic currency it takes to repay foreign borrowing diminishes. To the extent that monetary policy in source countries reacts aggressively to low domestic growth but normalizes only after extended periods, especially in an era of low inflation, the capital flows to, and currency appreciation in, the emerging market could be substantial.[3] Anticipating that the future buying power of domestic firms that have borrowed in dollars will increase as the domestic currency appreciates, lenders will be willing to expand credit significantly to other domestic firms today. This leads to higher upfront borrowing and higher asset prices. This, however, also results in the corporate sector neglecting to attend to internal governance. Its debt capacity then becomes overly reliant on the continued availability of liquidity.

At some point, source country monetary policy will normalize—the third ingredient. Tighter source country policy will lead to a depreciating emerging market currency and thus lower rather than higher corporate liquidity. Moreover, leverage is much higher at the onset of tightening, because lenders have been anticipating a high probability of continued liquidity. Debt repayment and the capacity to roll over debt will fall, not just because liquidity is lower but because corporate governance has been neglected. The combination of high leverage and a plunge in debt capacity will mean domestic and foreign lenders will be reluctant to renew loans. If the corporate sector has substantial, preexisting short-term borrowing, the decline in debt capacity can precipitate a run and thus force the firm immediately into distress.

While the collapse in prospective liquidity may originate with a change in the source country monetary stance, it need have nothing to do with macroeconomic policies in the emerging market and the credibility or lack thereof. Put differently, the boom and bust in the emerging market could be a genuine spillover from the source country policy. The so-called taper tantrum provides a good example of how a change in advanced economy monetary policy—or even the expectation of a change—creates fallout for emerging markets.

Why Standard Nostrums Do Not Work

Before the recent financial crisis, there was a sense among policymakers that the world had arrived at a policy optimum, which had contributed to a "great moderation" in economic volatility. In this world, the sole objective for monetary policy was domestic price stability, and it was achieved by flexible inflation targeting. By allowing the exchange rate to respond as needed, the system eliminated the need to intervene in currency markets or accumulate reserves. For instance, if capital flows came into a country, and the exchange rate were allowed to appreciate, eventually capital would stop flowing in as the prospect of future depreciation reduced expected returns.

A vast body of research since the Global Financial Crisis of 2007–2008 suggests this view is too complacent—the spillovers from capital inflows cannot be offset by allowing exchange rates to appreciate. Instead, many countries that did just that found yet more capital flowing in, chasing the returns that earlier investors had realized.[4]

Indeed, our model suggests fluctuations in the exchange rate are an important reason for fluctuations in corporate liquidity in capital receiving countries. Emerging market economies have often been accused of manipulating their currencies to make their exports more competitive. But worries about trade competitiveness need not be the only reason receiving-country authorities fear allowing their currency to float or move freely against the dollar. Our model suggests the "fear of floating" described by Hausmann, Panizza, and Stein (2001) and Calvo and Reinhart (2002) could really be a form of macroprudential policy: from the perspective of our model, a sustained appreciation lays the seeds for financial fragility, which then materializes in the event of a sharp depreciation. The authorities have seen the same movie many times and know how it ends, so they act prudentially by combating currency volatility.

Certainly, a number of emerging market countries have also understood that they should build foreign exchange reserves in the face of a sustained domestic currency appreciation. Since dollar weakness is the typical counterpart of domestic currency strength, such purchases across a number of emerging markets may be seen as a widespread demand for "safe" assets at such times. In reality, it is an attempt by receiving countries to slow currency appreciation, even while building a war chest to combat the inevitable depreciation. Hofmann, Shin, and Villamizar-Villegas (2019) offer evidence showing that exchange intervention smooths the growth of corporate borrowing, a fundamental prediction of our model. Of course, such intervention exacerbates moral hazard (corporations see a lower risk of borrowing in foreign currency once the central bank smooths currency volatility), which is why some emerging markets like China and India try and control corporate foreign borrowing also.

Unfortunately, there are few other tools that authorities have that will not disrupt the domestic economy significantly. Importantly, tighter monetary policy in the receiving country risks shifting the currency composition of corporate borrowing yet further into "cheaper" dollars (and exacerbating the domestic exchange appreciation), while more accommodative policy could encourage excessive domestic credit expansion.

The tendency for booms and busts in receiving countries becomes more pronounced as quiescent inflation makes source country monetary policy accommodative over long periods, as has been the case in recent decades before the pandemic.[5] From the receiving country's perspective, a commitment to "low for long" in the source country is a commitment to sustained easy liquidity in the receiving country—until it reverses. This implies a substantial buildup in leverage and financial fragility. No wonder a variety of emerging market policy makers have expressed concern both at sustained easy policy in source countries, as well as the possibility that these are reversed abruptly. These concerns are not in contradiction; one follows from the other.

Note: Since the Karl Brunner lecture was delivered, Bergant, Mishra, and Rajan (2023) test the details of the model just laid out, and find evidence consistent with it.

Scope for Multilateral Action

What responsibility do source countries have for these spillovers? The view that spillovers resulted primarily from insufficient exchange rate adjustment in recipient countries suggested there was none. This is indeed the view that some advanced economy central bankers, focused on their domestic mandates, espouse. It is hard to know whether they would have the same view if their mandates also included some element of international responsibility. Others recognize there may be spillovers but do not see any possibility of altering the behavior of sending countries. Instead, they focus on so-called macroprudential policies and capital flow measures in recipient countries, as does the IMF.[6] Yet macroprudential policy is narrow in scope—often the macroprudential authorities have jurisdiction over only parts of the financial system while monetary policy, as Jeremy Stein has argued, gets "into all the cracks." Macroprudential policies are also yet to show their effectiveness. The broader point is not to rule out the use of macroprudential tools but to emphasize that they are largely untried and cannot be the fallback whenever there are suggestions that monetary policy needs to address broader concerns.

Some economists have called for monetary policy rules that constrain the actions of sending-country central banks under some circumstances—I will present some possibilities in chapter 3. For instance, certain kinds of unconventional monetary policy actions in specific environments could be ruled out of order because of the large adverse spillovers they create—much as sustained one-directional intervention in the exchange rate was frowned upon until recently. Adhering to such rules would not be a matter of altruism. Countries that have signed up to the IMF Articles of Agreement already accept responsibility for the international consequence of their actions. Such rules would limit central bank behavior under extreme circumstances without changing their mandates or requiring international coordination. Central banks would then simply avoid policies that transgress the rules. Indeed, an Eminent Persons Group, tasked by the G-20 with suggesting changes to the global financial architecture, has noted the need for a "rules-based international framework, drawing on a comprehensive and evolving evidence base . . . to provide policy advice through which countries seek to avoid policies with large spillovers, develop resilient markets, and benefit from capital flows while managing risks to financial stability."[7] It adds that the IMF should develop a framework that enables sending countries "to meet their domestic objectives while avoiding large international spillovers."

There is another intriguing possibility. Our model suggests that a long period of easy monetary policy could enhance leverage, inflate asset prices, and increase risks to the source country's *own* financial stability. If central bank monetary policies in source countries included a domestic financial stability mandate, policy actions might well be altered in a way that also mitigates external spillovers. I will return to this in the conclusion.

3 Rules of the Monetary Game

In chapter 2, we saw one-way monetary policy in source countries could spill over across borders via capital flows, as well as exchange rate and asset price movements. More generally, the financial world has become much more integrated through cross-border trade, investment, payments, and capital flows. Even so, central bank objectives and responsibilities continue to be entire domestic. Clearly, there is no domestic political payoff for politicians to expand their central bank's responsibilities. Furthermore, central bankers themselves do not want to incorporate the complications of accounting for the international spillovers of their actions into what is already a difficult job. And so long as the consequences of volatile capital flows are borne by emerging markets and developing countries while reserve currency countries find external outlets for yield-hungry capital, there really is no powerful constituency for change. This, then, is the problem that everyone is aware of but no one really wants to address.

Clearly, the issues are difficult to address even if there were a willingness to do so. And with the likely advent of central bank digital currencies and global stable coins, when capital flows will become even more rapid, matters will get yet more difficult. Prachi Mishra from the IMF[1] and I wrote the following piece to explore the issues involved and ask how one might arrive at new rules of the game. At this stage, we thought it wise to pay only a little attention to political feasibility—often developments, including turmoil and crisis, make the unthinkable possible. Instead, our focus is on technical feasibility: do we really know enough to set concrete rules and, if not, how should we proceed.

In order to avoid the destructive beggar-thy-neighbor strategies that emerged during the Great Depression, the postwar Bretton Woods regime attempted to prevent countries from depreciating their currencies to gain an unfair and sustained competitive advantage. The system required fixed, but occasionally adjustable, exchange rates and restricted cross-border capital flows. These elaborate rules on when a country could move its exchange rate peg gave way, in the post–Bretton Woods world of largely flexible exchange rates, to a free-for-all where the only proscribed activity was sustained unidirectional intervention by a country in its exchange rate, especially if it was running a current account surplus. For more normal policies, a widely held view at that time was that each country, doing what was best for itself in a regime of mobile capital, would end up doing what was best for the global equilibrium. For instance, a country trying to unduly depreciate its exchange rate through aggressive monetary policy would see inflation rise to offset any temporary competitive gains. However, even if such automatic adjustment did ever work, and our paper does not take a position on this, the global environment has changed. In the environment that prevailed between the Global Financial Crisis and the pandemic, we had:

- Weak aggregate demand, in part because of poorly understood consequences of population aging and productivity slowdown
- A more integrated and open world with large capital flows
- Significant government and private debt burdens
- Sustained low inflation

In such an environment, which could return in the future, the pressure to avoid overly low inflation, as well as the need to restore growth to reduce domestic unemployment, could cause a country's authorities to place more of a burden on unconventional monetary policies (UMPs) as well as on exchange rate or financial market interventions. These may have large adverse spillover effects on other countries. The domestic mandates of most central banks do not legally allow them to take the full extent of adverse spillovers abroad into account and may force them to undertake aggressive policies so long as they have some small, positive domestic effect. Consequently, the world may embark on a suboptimal collective path. We need to reexamine rules of the game to ensure responsible policy in such a context. This chapter suggests some of the issues that need to be considered.

The Problem with the Current System

All monetary policies have external spillover effects. If a country reduces domestic interest rates, its exchange rate also typically depreciates, helping exports. Under normal circumstances, the "demand-creating" effects of lower interest rates on domestic consumption and investment are not small relative to the "demand-switching" effects of the lower exchange rate in enhancing external demand for the country's goods. Indeed, one could argue that the spillovers to the rest of the world could be positive on net, as the enhanced domestic demand draws in substantial imports, offsetting the higher exports at the expense of other countries.

Matters have been less clear in the post–financial crisis world and with the unconventional monetary policies countries have adopted. For instance, if the interest rate–sensitive segments of the economy are constrained by existing debt, lower rates may have little effect on enhancing domestic demand but continue to have demand-switching effects through the exchange rate. Similarly, the unconventional "quantitative easing" policy of buying assets such as long-term bonds from domestic players may certainly lower long rates but may not have an effect on domestic investment if aggregate capacity utilization is low. Indeed, savers may respond to the increased distortion in asset prices by saving more. And if certain domestic institutional investors such as pension funds and insurance companies need high interest rates on long-term bonds to meet their future claims, they may respond by buying such bonds in less distorted markets abroad. Such a search for yield will depreciate the exchange rate. If so, the primary effect of this policy on domestic demand may be through the demand-switching effects of a lower exchange rate rather than through a demand-creating channel.[2]

Other countries can react to the consequences of unconventional monetary policies, and some economists argue that it is their unwillingness to react appropriately—for instance, by tightening policy or allowing domestic exchange rate appreciation—that is the fundamental problem.[3] Yet concerns about monetary and financial stability may prevent those countries, especially less institutionally developed ones, from reacting to offset the disturbance emanating from the initiating country (see chapters 1 and 2 in this volume). It seems reasonable that a globally responsible assessment of policies should take the world as it is, rather than as a hypothetical ideal.

Ultimately, if all countries engage in demand-switching policies, we could have a race to the bottom. Countries may find it hard to get out of such policies because the immediate effect for the country that exits might be a serious appreciation of the exchange rate and a fall in domestic activity. Moreover, as argued in the previous chapter, the consequences of unconventional policies over the medium term need not be benign if aggressive monetary easing results in distortions to asset markets and debt buildup, with an eventual disastrous denouement.

Thus far, we have focused on exchange and interest rate effects of a country's monetary policy on the rest of the world. An obviously related channel of transmission of a country's monetary policy to the rest of the world in the post–Bretton Woods system has been through capital flows. These have been prompted not just by interest differentials but also by changes in institutional attitudes toward risk and leverage, influenced by sending-country monetary policies. Post–Global Financial Crisis capital flows to emerging markets (EMs) have been large. This is despite great reluctance on the part of several EMs to avoid absorbing the inflows.

As a consequence, corporate leverage in emerging economies has increased significantly.[4] The increase could reflect the direct effect of cross-border banking flows, changes in global risk aversion stemming from source country monetary policy,[5] the promise of abundant future liquidity on borrowing capacity (see chapter 2), or the indirect effects of an appreciating exchange rate and rising asset prices, which may make it seem that emerging market borrowers have more equity than they really have.[6]

The unintended consequence of such flows is that they are significantly influenced by the monetary policies of the sending countries and may reverse quickly—as they did during the taper tantrum in 2013. This means that they are not a reliable source of financing, which then requires emerging market central banks to build ample stocks of liquidity (that is, foreign exchange reserves) for when the capital flows reverse. Moreover, the liquidity insurance provided by emerging market central banks to their borrowers is never perfect, so when capital flows reverse, they tend to leave financial and economic distress in their wake. Capital flows, driven or pulled back by the monetary policy stance in industrial countries, create risk on the way in and distress on the way out. They constitute both a costly spillover and a significant constraint on emerging market monetary flexibility.

The bottom line is that simply because a policy is called monetary, unconventional, or otherwise, it may not be beneficial on net for the world. That all monetary policies have external spillovers does not mean that they are all justified. What matters is the relative magnitude of demand-creating versus demand-switching effects and the magnitude of other financial sector spillovers, that is, the net spillovers.[7]

Of course, a central contributor today to policymakers putting lower weight on international spillovers is that almost all central banks have purely domestic mandates. If they are in danger of violating the lower bound of their inflation mandate, for example, they are required to adopt all possible policies to get inflation back on target, no matter what their external effect. Indeed, they can even intervene directly in the exchange rate in a sustained and unidirectional way, although internationally, this could be seen as an abdication of international responsibility according to the old standards. The current state of affairs means that central banks find all sorts of ways to justify their policies in international fora without acknowledging the unmentionable—that the exchange rate may be the primary channel of transmission and external spillovers may be significantly adverse. Unfortunately, even if they do not want to abdicate international responsibility, their domestic mandates may give them no other options. In what follows, we will examine sensible rules of monetary behavior assuming the domestic mandate does not trump international responsibility.

Principles for Setting New Rules

Monetary policy actions by one country can lead to measurable and significant cross-border spillovers. If such spillovers are ignored, countries may undertake domestically optimal policies that have costs for other countries. If countries agree on a set of new rules or principles that describe the limits of acceptable behavior, they can reduce inefficiencies, leading to better global outcomes. This does not mean countries have to coordinate policies, only that they have to become better global citizens in foregoing policies that have large negative external effects. We had one such rule in the past—no sustained unidirectional intervention in the exchange rate—but with the plethora of new unconventional policies, we have to find new, clear, and mutually acceptable rules.

What would be the basis for the new rules? As a start, policies could be broadly rated based on analytical inputs and discussion. To use a driving analogy, polices that have few adverse spillovers and are even to be encouraged by the global community could be rated green, policies that should be used temporarily and with care could be rated orange, and policies that should be avoided at all times could be rated red. We will discuss the broad principles for such ratings in this section and whether economist's tools today allow empirical analysis to provide a clear-cut rating of policies. (To preview the answer, it is "No!") We will then argue that it may still be possible to make progress, once broad principles of the sort discussed in this section are agreed on.

A number of issues would need to be considered in developing a framework to rate policies.

- Should a policy that has any adverse spillovers outside the country of origin be totally avoided? Or should the benefits in the country of origin be added to measure the net global effects of the policy? In other words, should we consider the enhancement to global welfare or only the net spillovers to others in judging policy?

- Should the measurement of spillovers take into account any policy reactions by other countries? In other words, should the policy be judged based on its partial equilibrium or general equilibrium effects?

- Should domestic benefits weigh more and adverse spillovers weigh less for countries that have run out of policy options and have been stuck in slow growth for a long time? Should countries be allowed "jumpstarts" even if they impose costs on others?

- Should spillovers be measured over the medium term or evaluated at a point in time?

- Should spillovers (both positive and negative) be weighted more heavily for poorer countries that have weaker institutions and less effective policy instruments?

- Should spillovers be weighted by the affected population or by the dollar value of the effect?

Some tentative answers follow.

In general, policies that have net adverse outside spillovers over time could be rated red and should be avoided. Such policies obviously include those that have small positive effects in the home country (where the policy action originates) combined with large negative effects in the foreign country (where the spillovers occur). For example, if unconventional monetary policy actions lead to a feeble recovery in some of the advanced countries by facilitating exports to EMs but also lead to large capital flows to, and asset price bubbles in, the EMs, these policies could be rated red. Global welfare would decrease with this policy.

If a policy has positive effects on both home and foreign countries, and therefore on global welfare, it would definitely be rated green. Conventional monetary policy would fall in this category, as it would raise output in the home economy and create demand for exports from the foreign economy. A green rating for such policies would, however, assume that the stage of the financial and credit cycle in the home and foreign economies is such that financial stability risks from low interest rates are likely to be limited.[8]

It is possible to visualize other policies that have large positive effects for the originating country (because of the value of the policy or because of the country's relative size) and sustained small negative effects for the rest of the world. Global welfare, crudely speaking, may go up with the policy, even though welfare outside the originating country goes down. While it is hard to rate such policies without going into specifics, these may correctly belong in the orange category: permissible for some time but not on a sustained basis. Even conventional monetary policies to raise growth in the home economy could fall in the orange category if countries are at a financial stage where low interest rates lead to significant financial stability risks in the foreign economies.

Clearly, foreign countries may have policy room to respond, and that should be taken into account. So, for instance, a home country A at the zero lower bound may initiate quantitative easing (QE), and a foreign country B may respond by cutting interest rates to avoid capital inflows and exchange rate appreciation. The spillover effects of QE would be based on B's welfare if QE were not undertaken versus B's welfare after QE is initiated and it responds.

A policy could also be rated green if it acts as a booster shot for an economy stuck in a rut and if it can jumpstart that economy but creates temporary negative spillovers for foreign economies (for example, Lars Svensson's proposal for Japan to engage in exchange rate targeting in order to alter inflationary expectations).[9] Even if there are temporary adverse spillovers on foreign countries, the policy—through its effect on home economy growth and demand for foreign goods—can eventually provide offsetting large positive spillovers to the rest of the world. Of course, it is important that the home economy, after receiving the booster shot and picking up growth, not follow policies (such as holding down its exchange rate longer term) that minimize positive spillovers to other countries. A policy rated red on a static basis could thus be deemed green based on commitments over time. This also means that policies should be rated over the medium term rather than on the basis of one-shot static effects.

What we have just argued is that countries stuck in a rut for a long time and with few other options should temporarily be allowed policies that may have adverse spillovers. But what if the policy is sought to be employed over the medium term? Here, "rut" is a relative term both over time and across countries. If a stagnant rich country is allowed a free pass, should historically stagnant poor countries have a permanent pass to do whatever is in their best interests? It would be difficult to carve out exceptions to developed countries based on relative stagnation, or deviations from trend growth, without admitting a whole lot of other exceptions.

In this vein, poorer countries typically have weaker institutions—for example, central banks with limited credibility and budgetary frameworks that are not constrained by rules and watchdogs. As a result, their ability to offset spillovers with policies is typically more limited. Furthermore, poorer citizens live closer to the minimum margin of sustainability, and poorer countries typically have weaker safety nets. So there is a case for weighting spillovers to poor countries more. However, it will be difficult to determine precisely what weight to place. Nevertheless, this facet could be kept in mind in deciding how to rate a policy when it is on the borderline.

A related problem is whether spillovers should be measured in aggregate monetary terms or in "utils" weighted by population. Once again, determining utility may be hard, so perhaps at first pass, it may be better to evaluate the dollar value of spillovers without attempting a further translation in utility. This will certainly facilitate adding up across countries and over time to see the net effect of policies.

Overall, whether policies are rated red, green, or orange would depend on a number of factors such as the stage of the financial and business cycle in the home and foreign countries, whether the policy action constitutes a booster shot to jumpstart the economy or gives only a mild boost and has to be employed for a sustained period, whether standard transmission channels are clogged so that unconventional policies are warranted, whether the foreign country has room to adopt buffering policies, whether the spillovers affect poor countries that have weak institutions and less room to respond, and so on.

Finally, some examples of policies that could be rated could include the following:

- Direct or "evident" exchange rate manipulation (e.g., through massive intervention in the foreign exchange market, which aims to depreciate a country's exchange rate or not let it appreciate, or keep it "undervalued" relative to some benchmark).

- Other indirect policies that have large asset price or exchange rate effects with uncertain effects on real activity—unconventional monetary policies might fall within this categorization.

- Policies that can have financial sector spillovers such as facilitating capital flows, high credit growth, and asset price bubbles. These could also be considered as generating large adverse spillovers through the financial system. Low interest rate policies for extremely long periods in advanced economies could fall in this category.

Before concluding this section, let us address five common reactions to any suggestion of rules of the game.

Central banks already take into account spillback effects of their policies, even if they have a domestic mandate. This is true, but the spillback effects (the partial consequences of their policies as they flow back to the source country, for example, through the lower growth and thus lower imports of trading partners) may be only a fraction of the spillover effects. What matters for the world as a whole is that countries internalize spillover effects.

Central banks already discuss their policies at various forums and strive to communicate and be transparent. Yes, but open communication and transparency still are tantamount to saying, "It's our policy, and your problem."

Taking spillover effects into account would make policymaking, which is already hard, overly complicated and impossible to communicate. Yes, but presumably countries already take spillback effects into account, which involves estimating policy reaction functions of other countries. How much more complicated will it be to take spillover effects into account?

Rules will constrain only the systemically important central banks. Probably, although smaller countries will also have obligations. It is a reality that the consequences of monetary policy are asymmetric and depend on a country's importance. Often, this is a source of privilege and power. We are suggesting some commensurate obligations.

Any rules will affect a central bank's ability to deliver on its domestic mandate. True, which is why we will eventually have to explore how domestic mandates sit with international obligations in this integrated world. In many other areas of international interaction (e.g., carbon emissions), we rarely argue that a country is free to do what is best domestically even if it imposes costs on the rest of the world. It cannot be that monetary policy gets a free pass simply because monetary mandates were put in place when spillovers were less of a concern.

There is a fast-growing empirical literature on estimating spillovers.[10] Much of it seems to have focused on analyzing the international transmission of outcome variables like government bond yields or exchange rates rather than measuring cross-border spillovers from specific policies. Where studies have tried to measure spillovers from specific policies, *identifying* the spillover effects remains a challenge.

Given this state of the art, it might not be wise to use the analysis as anything more than a basis of discussion to rate policies. Instead, many policies will fall in the orange zone, with much of the discussion about how further adjustments can take them well and truly into the green zone. Experience—and postmortem analysis—may indicate some policies should truly have been classified red. Over time, analysis plus experience can allow a sharper rating of policies.

How to Proceed?

The next crucial questions are as follows: Who should assess spillovers? What would be an appropriate forum to discuss spillover effects from specific policies and the ratings of these policies? How should we proceed?

A Group of Eminent Academics
Given the constraints and political difficulties under which international organizations operate, it may be appropriate to start with a group of eminent academics with reasonable representation across the globe and have them assess the spillovers and grade policies. They could offer periodic assessments back to the central bankers who gather at the Bank for International Settlements in Basel.

International Meetings
Once central bankers have some confidence, perhaps the next step would be to involve other policymakers by discussing international spillover effects at meetings such as those of the IMF Board, the International Monetary and Financial Committee, and the G20. The discussion would be based on background papers, which would be commissioned from both traditional sources like the IMF and nontraditional sources like the group of academics and EM central banks.

These papers would attempt to isolate the nature of spillovers as well as their magnitude and attempt a preliminary classification of policy actions. Almost surely, there will be a lot of fuzziness about which color to attribute to a wide range of recent policies. But discussion can help participants understand both how the policies could be classified if we had better models and data and how the models and data gathering can be improved.

Country Responsibilities before Formal Rules
When policies are being discussed so as to get better understanding, no policies that affect the international monetary system should be off the table. Importantly, simply denoting a policy with the label "monetary" should not give it an

automatic free pass because it falls under the central bank's domestic mandate. What will be important is not the policy-maker's mandate, professed intent, or instruments but actual channels of transmission and outcomes, including spillovers. Policymakers should be encouraged to respond to the back-ground papers by stating and explaining their policy actions, attempting to persuade the international community that they fall in the green and orange zones.

International Conference

As the international community builds understanding on what constitutes sensible rules of the game and how to label policies in that context, perhaps an international conference may be warranted to see how the community's understanding of beneficial rules can be implemented. At that time, a discus-sion of how a central bank's international responsibilities fit in with its domestic mandate may be warranted. While rec-ognizing the political difficulty of altering any central bank's mandate, the conference will have to deliberate on how inter-national responsibilities can be woven into existing mandates. It will have to decide whether a new international agreement along the lines of Bretton Woods is needed or whether much can be accomplished by small changes in the Fund's Articles of Agreement, accompanied by corresponding changes in man-dates of country authorities.

Role of the Fund

What role would the International Monetary Fund play? The obligations of members and the authority of the Fund are derived from the Articles of Agreement. Section 1 of Article IV makes clear that IMF members are under general obliga-tion "to collaborate with other members of the Fund to assure orderly exchange arrangements and to promote a stable system of exchange rates." The meaning of "general obligation" is unclear in the Articles but could be "relied upon as a basis for the Fund to call on its members to take specific actions or to refrain from taking specific actions."[11] Article IV further states, "In particular, each member shall . . . (iii) avoid manipulating exchange rates or the international monetary system in order to prevent effective balance of payments adjustment or to gain unfair competitive advantage over other members." Furthermore, the Principles for the Guidance of Members' Exchange Rate Policies (originally 1977, amended in 2007) note, "Members should take into account in their intervention policies the interests of other members, including those in whose currency they intervene."

Although the Articles of Agreement or the Principles do not define "manipulation" in any detail, IMF (2007) narrows the scope of manipulation by noting that "manipulation of the exchange rate is only carried through policies that are targeted at—and actually affect—the level of exchange rate. Moreover, manipulation may cause the exchange rate to move or may prevent such movement."

In practice, it may be difficult to determine if a policy is targeted at attaining a level of exchange rate. Direct policy actions such as intervention in the foreign exchange market or indirect policies such as monetary, fiscal, and trade policies or regulations of capital movements, regardless of the intent or purpose, can also affect the level of the exchange rate and can be interpreted as "manipulation." The interpretation of the Articles of Agreement could perhaps be broadened in scope to include a wider range of policies that can primarily have effects on the exchange rates and therefore beggar-thy-neighbor consequences.

While the Articles of Agreement include members' obligations in relation to exchange rate policies, global financial stability implications of country-specific policies are not touched upon anywhere in the Articles. Members' obligations are considered only in relation to domestic growth objectives. For example, based on the Articles, a country with a weak economy can pursue loose monetary policies to stimulate output and employment. Despite the implications of such policies for financial stability in other countries, the country would argue that its policies are in line with Article IV, Section 1(i), which allows each member to "direct its economic and financial policies toward the objective of fostering orderly economic growth with reasonable price stability." More generally, the Fund's Articles may need altering based on the discussion of the rules of the game.

Moreover, although broader surveillance by the Fund of its members' exchange rate policies and other policies with significant financial sector spillovers (and perhaps public statements about such policies) can help alert investors to possible adverse effects, countries are not obligated to follow Fund advice unless in a program. The more pertinent question, therefore, might be: What can the Fund really do once its executive board determines that a particular country is in violation of its obligations under the new rules of the game? An optimistic view is that the clear focus on the downsides of the particular country's actions for the rest of the world will lead to political and economic pressures from around the world that make the country cease and desist. The clearer the eventual rules of the game, the more likely this outcome will be. Realistically, though, the world's experience with moral suasion (or name and shame) as a way to get countries to behave has, at best, been mixed. Regardless, we are so far from agreed-on rules that contemplating enforcement at this point seems premature.

Conclusions

As this paper suggests, there is much that needs to be pinned down on the international spillovers from domestic policies. With economic analysis of these issues at an early stage, it is unlikely we will get strong policy prescriptions soon, let alone international agreement on them, especially given that a number of country authorities—like central banks—have explicit domestic mandates.

This paper therefore suggests a period of focused discussion, first outside international meetings and then within international meetings. A discussion of the international spillovers of domestic policies need not take place in an environment of finger-pointing and defensiveness but as an attempt to craft reasonable, and not overly intrusive, rules of conduct.

As consensus builds on the rules of conduct, we can contemplate the next step of whether to codify them through international agreement, and we can see how the Articles of multilateral watchdogs like the IMF will have to be altered and how country authorities will interpret or alter domestic mandates to incorporate international responsibilities.

Obviously, any attempt to strengthen international rules in the current environment where countries are growing increasingly nationalistic and turning away from international responsibilities could be seen as optimistic at best and naive at worst. We must, however, keep in mind two developments that make reform urgent. First, the increase in cross-border flows, especially as technical innovations like central bank digital currencies and global stable coins take hold, makes the world ever more integrated. Second, the world is becoming multipolar. The system worked in the past despite the absence of rules because it had one hegemon, the United States, who broadly influenced behavior in the system. As the economic world becomes more multipolar, and as rising powers reject the current system as overly favorable to the dominant powers of the past, the risk of conflicts over behavior increases. With no single hegemon to police the system, it will probably work better if there are broadly accepted rules that bind every large player. This paper is an attempt to start the dialogue toward reaching consensus on an acceptable set of rules.

4   Central Banking, Political Pressure, and Its Unintended Consequences

In 2020, the world was hit by a devastating pandemic, which prompted a massive monetary and fiscal response. From a situation of too-low inflation that I described in previous chapters, industrial country central banks found inflation uncomfortably high. Unfortunately, the central banking policies followed over the previous decades meant that economies were far less prepared for a tough fight against inflation. Nearly a decade after I delivered my Andrew Crockett Lecture (chapter 1), I take stock of what we have learned about unconventional monetary policy. The passage of time has only increased my conviction that, as with most actions, monetary policy is best conducted with moderation and with humility about the possible unintended consequences of policy. This chapter is based on my keynote address at the Cato Institute's 39th Annual Monetary Conference, November 18, 2021.

The proper role of central banks, the frameworks they use, and the range of tools they believe they can legitimately employ have changed considerably over the past two decades. Interestingly, this has come after perhaps their greatest triumph, taming inflation. What led to this rethinking? And what are its consequences, some possibly unintended? What have been the effects on financial stability? These are the questions this final chapter examines.

To preview my answers, central bankers escaped lightly from
the Global Financial Crisis (GFC), getting little of the blame
but acquiring an aura of possessing extraordinary powers as
they helped resolve the crisis. One consequence, however, may
have been more public calls for central banks to deliver for
Main Street. As they subsequently and continuously undershot
their inflation target, the pressure on them to aid economic
activity increased. Perhaps tinged somewhat with hubris, central banks did not reject these pressures and make the case
that there are limits to what central banks can properly do.
Instead, they embraced the challenge and embarked on a much
broader set of interventions, including direct interventions in
asset and credit markets that they eschewed in the past.

Arguably, these interventions have not helped central
banks much in achieving their inflation targets. Instead, they
have left them poorly positioned for an environment where
fiscal spending has ramped up and inflation, not disinflation,
is the key problem. Furthermore, central banks have continued underemphasizing financial stability throughout this
time, which also leaves the world poorly positioned for future
shocks, including from the changing climate. In trying to do
too much, central banks have not just compromised on their
fundamental responsibility, price stability, but also added to
financial instability. In sum, this article is a call for central
banks to go back to the knitting and reassess both their goals
as well as their use of tools.

A Short History of the Recent Evolution
of Central Banking Thought

The actions of the Federal Reserve, no doubt influenced by
developments in academia and by the actions of other central

banks, have broadly framed the consensus in central bank thinking. After all, it was Paul Volker's determination to push short-term nominal interest rates really high and hold them there until inflation came down that broke the back of US inflation, raised the Fed's credibility as an inflation fighter, and contributed to decades of falling nominal interest rates. Kydland and Prescott's (1977) theory of time inconsistency of policy and the need for commitment, as well as Rogoff's (1985) arguments on how to achieve that commitment through an independent, inflation-minded central bank, made the case for central bank independence. The Bank of New Zealand, in turn, became the first central bank to formally adopt inflation targeting in 1990, and this spread across the world. Meanwhile, John Taylor (1993) described central bank behavior with a simple model that then became the standard for evaluating whether a central bank was ahead or behind the curve in its fight against inflation. Indeed, so remarkable was the worldwide fall in inflation that Rogoff (2004) suggested that it could not just be attributed to central bank independence and policy and conjectured that global competition must also have helped.

Be that as it may, with inflation quiescent over long periods, central banks no longer had to raise interest rates periodically. As Borio (2014a) notes, this allowed the financial cycle—the unwholesome correlated increases in asset prices and leverage—to play out over longer periods and with greater amplitude. In this article, I argue there are many channels through which more accommodative monetary policy can initiate and propagate such a cycle. For instance, as interest rates fall, long-term expectations of growth account for a larger and larger share in asset valuations. Given there is little to anchor such expectations, a wide distribution of valuations is possible. The more optimistic among potential buyers buy more long-dated assets financed with borrowing.[1] Their wealth is further enhanced by falling rates, allowing them to exercise more of an influence in setting asset prices. Sustained periods of low and falling inflation could thus be accompanied by optimistic asset prices, leverage, and risks to financial stability when prices and leverage correct.

In late 1996, Fed chairman Alan Greenspan came as close as a central banker can to saying he thought stock prices were overvalued and that the Fed would potentially take that into account in setting monetary policy.[2] Yet, his speech warning of "irrational exuberance," at the American Enterprise Institute on December 5, was shrugged off by markets—and markets were right. The Fed did not act, perhaps warned off by the vociferous political reaction to his speech. The Fed watched while stock prices continued rising during the internet boom and even cut rates following the Russian debt default in 1998 and the collapse of hedge fund Long-Term Capital Management.

When the stock market eventually crashed in 2000, the Fed responded by cutting rates, ensuring the recession was mild even if subsequent job growth was tepid. In a 2002 speech at the Kansas City Fed's Jackson Hole Conference, Alan Greenspan argued that, while the Fed could not recognize or prevent asset price booms, it could "mitigate the fallout when it occurs and, hopefully, ease the transition to the next expansion."[3] His speech seemed to be a post-facto rationalization of why he had not acted more forcefully on his prescient 1996 intuition. He was now saying the Fed should not intervene when it thought asset prices were too high but that the Fed could recognize a bust when it happened and would pick up the pieces. Given that inflation was quiescent, the resulting monetary policy was asymmetrical. The Fed would take little action other than a normalization of interest rates when the economy was booming but take increasingly aggressive actions to support the economy when activity (and, not coincidentally) asset prices were down. Effectively, the Fed offered traders and bankers a "put option," whereby if they collectively gambled on similar things, the Fed would not limit the upside, but if their bets turned sour, the Fed would limit the downside.

Clearly, no central bank wants such asymmetric incentives, yet with one interest rate tool, central banks believed they could not simultaneously achieve both monetary and financial stability. Therefore, it was left to an often poorly defined set of macroprudential policies to curb risk taking. It was convenient for the powerful monetary policy setting arms of central banks to delegate this messy task to someone else. It was also dangerous for the system. First, as Kohn (2015) points out, even today the Fed has no central body with macroprudential responsibility. This is particularly problematic since macroprudential regulation has the politically difficult task of constraining risk taking just when the risk takers have tasted success and are more influential. When responsibility is diffused, it is all too easy to leave action to someone else. Second, as Stein (2013) points out, vast areas of the financial system are regulated lightly, if at all. Macroprudential regulation has little bite there. The value of monetary action is that "it gets into all the cracks."

Be that as it may, the Global Financial Crisis of 2007–2009 was evidence that the system of divided responsibilities did not work. No doubt, bank regulation has improved considerably since then, and banks are much better supervised, capitalized, and incentivized than before the GFC. Yet the nonbank periphery of the financial system, also termed the "shadow financial system," continues to have considerably less oversight or regulation, and risks tend to migrate there, periodically coming back to ensnare the banking system—as evidenced by recent blowups such as Archegos or Greensill. With the rise of cryptocurrencies, stablecoins, and decentralized finance, the size and complexity of the unregulated shadow system have only grown.

Further offsetting the post-GFC increased bank regulation is the fact that, post-GFC, central banks have not been achieving their inflation targets and therefore have come under greater pressure to be aggressively accommodative on monetary policy. For instance, in the United States, personal consumption expenditure (PCE) inflation, the Fed's preferred measure, averaged about 1.4 percent from 2012 to 2020, below the 2 percent target. That policy interest rates were at the zero lower bound seemed to be no defense. From the political side, pressure on the central bank mounted in a time of low growth. If the central bank is not meeting its target, there must be some stimulus it is not delivering, or so the thinking went. As the European Central Bank (ECB) realized over 2010–2013, pressure to do something could also come from an appreciating exchange rate, as other central banks found new, innovative ways of easing financing conditions.

But central bankers did not also reject their own responsibility for excessively low inflation, perhaps because they were worried about losing credibility if they claimed they had done all they could. They always seemed to suggest they had more tools to push inflation up, even after repeated failures. Indeed, one can discern a hint of smugness in their lament that fiscal policy and reforms were not working, and monetary policy was the "only game in town." But while Volker had taught central banks how to bring down inflation, there was no obvious playbook for reflating an economy, especially when nominal rates were already at zero and fiscal policy limited.

How Did Monetary Policy Change after the GFC?

Following the Global Financial Crisis, with interest rates at zero, further unconventional monetary interventions took three broad forms: repairing markets, altering asset prices, and direct credit programs. At the core of all these was a greater willingness of the central bank to intervene in markets.

Repairing Markets

A number of financial markets had broken down during the GFC. Some of this was due to lack of confidence, some to lack of liquidity, and some because key players were undercapitalized. Of course, there was also a possibility that some of the financial claims being traded were worthless because the issuers were insolvent. Nevertheless, central banks attempted to alter perceptions and engender a virtuous circle by intervening. The hope was that the restoration of public confidence through the central bank's support of financial markets, coupled with the liquidity injected through purchases, would recapitalize market players, increase their participation, and restore asset values and trading volume to asset markets. In its first round of quantitative easing (QE1), the Fed invested in the disrupted mortgage-backed securities (MBS) market while the ECB, through its "outright monetary transactions" policy, backed sovereign bonds of periphery governments.[4] Whether the central bank changed perceptions of market fundamentals, or whether it drew attention to put options that it had implicitly written for these markets, is hard to tell. Regardless, the interventions seem to have restored transaction volumes and prices to more normal levels, ensuring their place in future toolkits.

Altering Asset Prices

Monetary policy works, in part, by signaling the path of short-term interest rates and therefore affecting long-term interest rates. With policy rates at zero, and with little room to cut them further, central banks looked for other ways to affect long-term rates more directly. One way was to expand central bank balance sheets through an announced program of buying long-term government bonds, with the intent of depressing long-term interest rates. Whether this worked (if it worked at all) by taking long-term assets out of private hands and forcing private portfolios to rebalance by buying more long-term assets or by committing that policy rates would not be raised so long as the central bank is buying long-term assets is unclear.[5,6] Other central banks such as the Bank of Japan practiced "yield curve control," where they sought to keep the yield of a specific bond such as the ten-year bond at a targeted level through direct central bank purchases or sales of the bond. While the effects of such interventions on long-term rates were much clearer, there was no compelling evidence that those efforts helped enhance real investment or economic activity.

Of course, there were parallels between various forms of QE and the discredited past direct financing of governments by their captive central banks. Monetary economists used to frown on this practice because the central bank essentially gave the government a "soft budget constraint," which proved to be inflationary. Central bank independence required them to stop financing governments directly. What distinguished the new central bank asset purchase programs from the discredited programs of the past was a fig leaf and circumstances. The fig leaf was that the central bank typically purchased in the secondary market, not directly from the government, although once the program was announced, markets anticipated such purchases, and this was a distinction without a difference. However, after the GFC, the circumstances were different from the typical situation where central bank financing of government debt is problematic. Interest rates were at the zero lower bound, and developed country governments were typically not strapped for cash, so central bank financing was not critical for their budgets.

I say "typically" because European periphery countries were indeed strapped. With the onset of the pandemic, this has become the case with more governments, and central banks have become key players in bridging government financing gaps.

Directed Credit Programs

Another element in the new toolkit was central bank participation in providing cheap refinancing for any bank credit that met specific conditions—loans to small and medium firms, households, or sometimes even any loan expansion at all. Once again, this cheap refinancing for bank credit revived old practices abandoned by central banks, which had argued that *directed credit* distorted the working of the capital markets and could lead to the political rather than market allocation of resources. Worries about distortions and politicization seemed minor when set against the enormity of the post-GFC economic downturn. One again, direct credited programs were revived and expanded following the onset of Covid-19 in March 2020.

Did These Policies Work?

At a narrow level, some of these unconventional policies seemed to work in that some of the stated intent was met. For instance, the MBS market recovered. Di Maggio, Kermani, and Palmer

(2020) show that Fed MBS purchases in what became known as QE1 led to an increase in refinancing, a reduction in mortgage payments, and an associated increase in consumption. Once again, whether the MBS market recovered because the central bank restored confidence (good) or because it offered the market a long-term put option (less good) is less clear.

Central bank actions did not always work as intended. Acharya et al. (2019) show that banks that held more European periphery sovereign bonds, when ECB President Mario Draghi boosted their value by announcing OMT, lent more. The effective recapitalization they obtained seemed to release constraints on lending. However, Acharya et al. (2019) argue that a number of the additional loans went to economically unviable "zombie" firms, whose continued financing and survival may have held back the recovery of industry. Central bank activism also "worked" at second or third remove, even when support was targeted. For instance, Grosse-Rueschkamp, Steffen, and Streitz (2019) show that ECB purchases of corporate bonds reduced yields for eligible firms, allowing them to repay bank debt with bond issuances—enabling banks to lend to riskier firms.

Of course, there is also evidence that central bank actions worked as intended. Foley-Fisher, Ramcharan, and Yu (2016), for example, offer evidence that the Fed's maturity extension program (also known as "Operation Twist") allowed firms dependent on long-term debt to issue more of it, expanding employment and investment.

Despite such positive micro-evidence, the broader macro-impacts, including on real activity, of these new central bank tools are harder to discern. Fabo et al. (2021) examine fifty-four studies on the effects of QE on output and inflation in the United States, United Kingdom, and the Euro area. While the papers by central bankers typically report a statistically significant QE effect on output, only half the academic papers do so. Interestingly, studies by the Bundesbank, a rare central bank opposed to QE, finds even smaller positive effects of QE on output than the academic papers. While it is inappropriate to conclude that central bank research is necessarily biased, the fact that specific assumptions can drive conclusions suggests that the evidence is fairly noisy—that is, the new policy tools did not offer overwhelming evidence of effectiveness.[7]

Why, then, did central banks embrace them? The nature of the tools suggests that post-GFC central banks had much less faith in the effective working of markets. Perhaps the markets' "irrational exuberance" was followed by irrational pessimism, with asset values significantly below true fundamentals. If so, central banks could put their balance sheets to work to correct misperceptions. Of course, there was always a danger that valuations would be altered, not because the market recognized true fundamentals but because the central bank intervention altered fundamentals. If true fundamentals eventually converged to central bank–altered fundamentals, the central bank might indeed be providing a valuable service. But if they did not converge, we would realize this only too late—when central banks did not have any further ability to expand their balance sheets to deliver on their contingent guarantees. Put differently, a key question today is, have central banks induced market dependence with their new tools and consequently tied their own actions to market performance?

Altering Frameworks

The Fed did more in the post-GFC low-inflation environment than just adopt unconventional tools. It also set about changing its framework so as to alter public expectations. Essentially, by committing to be more tolerant of inflation in the medium term, the Fed felt it would have greater credibility in signaling that interest rates would stay "lower for longer" even in the face of higher inflation. It would thus allow inflationary expectations to move higher. Put differently, the Fed had to erode some of its hard-won credibility for fighting high inflation in order to combat low inflation.

A key element of the Fed's new framework was that it would no longer be preemptive in heading off inflation. Instead, it would be measured and reactive.[8] The old Fed mantra—that if you are staring inflation in the eyeballs, it is already too late—was put to bed. Instead, the Fed would watch inflation rise until it had made up any shortfalls in past inflation, so that *average* inflation was around the target. Since the period over which the average was taken was undefined, the Fed could allow higher inflation for a while and not be criticized for falling behind the curve. Monetary policy could be more discretionary and could be used to meet a broader employment mandate, where unemployment not only had to be low but employment had to be broad based and inclusive. Since minorities unfortunately are last to be hired, this meant the Fed would potentially tolerate a tighter labor market than in the past. Finally, the Fed's employment mandate also became more asymmetric: rather than minimize deviations from maximum employment, it worried only about shortfalls now, leaving it to the now-more-accommodative inflation mandate to react to an overly tight labor market.

Isn't discretion good, especially for a professional apolitical organization? Possibly, but perhaps not when the environment changes in a way that was not envisaged by the framework and becomes vastly more politically charged, as I now argue.

What Changed?

Central banks were only partly responsible for the low-inflation environment over the past few decades. Part of the responsibility also lay with deeper structural forces affecting demand and supply, such as globalization, population aging, and rising income inequality within developed countries. But these also were changing.

One important prepandemic development was growing impediments placed on global trade and investment. Earlier, the rise of emerging markets, which were moving more workers from low-productivity agriculture into industry and service jobs, created a truly global goods and labor market. Greater competition reduced goods prices and wages, but a longer-lasting effect (which is what matters for inflation over the medium term) was, as Rogoff (2004) argues, that greater competition reduced central bank incentives to raise inflation to boost growth. However, with growing protectionism, trade disruption, and investment disputes between the two biggest economies in the world, borders are no longer as seamless as they once were. So even before the pandemic, the conditions holding down inflation were turning.

The pandemic further altered those conditions. Apart from the tragic and widespread loss of lives and livelihoods, the pandemic has disrupted the market for goods, services, and labor. The short-run disruptions will fade, and whether they will have lasting effects on the public's inflationary expectations is hard to tell. However, there are a number of channels through which the pandemic may have longer-lasting influences. The pandemic certainly seems to have led to a change in personal and public attitudes toward low-paying, low-benefit, precarious jobs. Such jobs have typically been on the pandemic frontline, involving high contact with people, long hours, and little job flexibility. Not only are workers reluctant to return to such jobs, but the public is also more supportive of higher pay and benefits for such work. More generally, wage demands are more likely to be accommodated in the postpandemic environment.

The pandemic has also increased the public's perception of the likelihood of tail events, increasing the political will behind combating climate change. This will imply higher costs of new investments, fully pricing emissions, and compliance with stricter regulations. Of course, these measures are needed. But if firms pass through the higher costs, which will likely come as a steady stream rather than as a one-off, they will also contribute to inflationary impulses.

Perhaps the biggest change in the pandemic response, relative to the response to the GFC, has been on the fiscal side. There are many possible explanations for the dramatic opening of fiscal taps across the world. These include the imperative for policymakers to act quickly, the need to obtain consensus in a sharply divided polity by spreading the benefits around, and the political pressure to expand fiscal deficits—driven perhaps by respectable economists whose convenient message (to politicians) seemed to be that developed countries could afford significantly more debt at current interest rates. Be that as it may, the consequence was a massive resource transfer to the private sector (i.e., to households, firms, and banks). In the United States, personal disposable income went up while bankruptcies fell during the pandemic, both firsts for what was ostensibly an economic downturn. Cash savings and pent-up demand have risen to extraordinary levels. With spending falling initially on goods, supply chains have become snarled. Of course, none of this need imply sustained inflation if the

central bank acts according to its mandate. There are, however, reasons why central banks will not simply bring out the
old Volkerian anti-inflation playbook.

Impediments to Policy Normalization

In the past, current levels of inflation would have prompted
central bankers to square their shoulders, look determinedly
into the TV cameras, and say, "We hate inflation, and we will
kill it"—or words to that effect. But now they are more likely
to make excuses for inflation, assuring the public that it will
simply go away. Clearly, the prolonged period of low inflation
after the Global Financial Crisis has had a lasting impression
on central bankers' psyches. The obvious danger now is that
they could be fighting the last war. Moreover, even if they do
not fall into that trap, structural changes within central banks
and in the broader policymaking environment will leave central bankers more reluctant to raise interest rates than they
were in the past. Consider why, focusing on the Fed.

Framework Dominance

As argued earlier, the Fed changed its framework to allow itself
to keep policies more accommodative for longer, believing it
was in an era of structurally low demand and weak inflation.
Ironically, the Fed may have given itself more flexibility just as
the economic regime itself was changing.

But shouldn't greater flexibility give decision makers more
options? Not necessarily. In the current scenario, Congress
has just spent trillions of dollars generating the best economic
recovery that money can buy. Imagine the congressional
wrath that would follow if the Fed now tanked the economy
by hiking interest rates without using the full flexibility of its

new framework. Put differently, one of the benefits of a clear inflation-targeting framework is that the central bank has political cover to react quickly to rising inflation. With the changed framework, that is no longer true. As a result, there will almost surely be more inflation for longer. Indeed, the new framework was adopted—during what now seems like a very different era—targeting precisely that outcome.

Market Dominance

But it is not just the new framework that limits the effectiveness of the Fed's actions. Anticipating loose monetary policy and financial conditions for the indefinite future, asset markets have been on a tear, supported by heavy borrowing. Market participants, rightly or wrongly, believe that the Fed has their back and will retreat from a path of rate increases if asset prices fall.

This means that when the Fed moves, it may have to raise rates higher in order to normalize financial conditions, implying a higher risk of an adverse market reaction when market participants finally realize that the Fed means business. Once again, the downside risks, both to the economy and to the Fed's reputation, of a path of rate hikes are considerable.

Fiscal Dominance

The original intent in making central banks independent of the government was to ensure that they could reliably combat inflation and not be pressured into either financing the government's fiscal deficit directly or keeping government borrowing costs low by slowing the pace of rate hikes. Yet the Fed now holds $5.6 trillion of government debt, financed by an equal amount of overnight borrowing from commercial banks.

When rates move up, the Fed itself will have to start paying higher rates, reducing the dividend it pays the government and increasing the size of the fiscal deficit. Moreover, US government debt is at around 125 percent of GDP, and a significant portion of it has a short-term maturity, which means that increases in interest rates will quickly start showing up in higher refinancing costs. An issue that the Fed did not have to pay much attention to in the past—the effects of rate hikes on the costs of financing government debt—will now be front and center.

Therefore, even as inflationary pressures rise, central banks are predisposed to waiting longer than in the past to see if they will simply go away. If the post-2008 scenario repeats, if new Covid-19 variants undermine growth, or if China and other emerging markets send disinflationary impulses across the global economy, waiting will have been the right decision. Otherwise, the present impediments to central bank action will mean more, and sustained, inflation and a more prolonged fight to control it. The problem is that a long period of monetary accommodation and diminished attention to financial stability while the problem of low inflation was being addressed have accentuated the financial cycle and exacerbated the risks to financial stability from tighter money.

Risks from a Prolonged Period of Accommodation

The economic system has gotten used to a period of very easy money. What are the risks when central banks do overcome the impediments that we just discussed and embark on policy normalization?

Untested Financial Innovation

There has been substantial financial innovation since the Global Financial Crisis—indeed, the dominant cryptocurrency, bitcoin, was conceived as a substitute to fiat currencies after the failure of Lehman Brothers, since central bankers could not be trusted to avoid the temptation of inflating away currency value. Innovative financial asset already have significant valuations and market shares but are untested through a serious downturn or through a normalization of monetary policy.

We will eventually learn answers to a number of questions. For instance, will credit be more available in a downturn because data substitute for collateral, or will it become more skewed because everyone coordinates on the same data and similar algorithms to avoid difficult credits? Will stablecoins experience traditional bank runs in a period of higher anxiety about valuations? How will loan losses shape up, and how easy will recoveries be on lending platforms and buy-now-pay-later schemes in a serious downturn? How will high-frequency trading affect prices then, and who will provide market-making services? It is unlikely that all the answers will be comforting.

Financial innovations can also enhance the speed of capital flows and thus traditional sources of fragility. For instance, countries with weak macroeconomic indicators and banking systems may see significantly more capital outflows in a period of rising interest rates than in the past, with cryptocurrencies offering new, effective channels for bypassing capital controls.

The point is that the shadow financial system has only grown since the GFC, and regulators, still using spreadsheets and pdf files, have to make significant strides to both understand financial innovations as well as how to regulate them, including through the use of technology.[9] The change in monetary environment may come before they are ready.

The High Level of Asset Prices

Periods of low rates inspire a search for yield from market participants with fixed nominal liabilities such as pension funds.[10] Rising asset prices, especially for innovative "alternative" asset classes, can also induce a fear of missing out among asset managers. Narratives about future use value, especially those with little falsifiability today, can imbue certain long-dated assets with high values when discounted at low long-term rates. How, for instance, will the value of cryptocurrencies, essentially long-dated, zero-coupon bonds priced on the hope they will dominate payments or be the new gold, adjust when interest rates move up? Given their value is cumulatively over $2.5 trillion on a good day, this is not an insignificant concern. What of a tech company, scheduled to make losses for the foreseeable future but priced at astronomical levels because, after all, Amazon made losses for a long time?

As argued earlier, the high level of asset prices can make the central bank's task in removing accommodation more difficult. If markets believe that the central bank will pause or reverse itself if prices fall, they may simply ignore the threat of higher policy rates. However, the price reaction, once markets understand the central bank is determined to remove accommodation, can be significant.

The key to whether asset price volatility leads to magnified real-sector volatility has to do with financial leverage. And high levels of asset prices both cause and are supported by high degrees of leveraging, as we saw in chapter 2.

Leverage

All manner of leverage—private, public, and market, explicit and implicit—has gone up since the GFC. As one example of disguised and implicit leverage, Archegos, a family office run by a convicted trader, was able to borrow about five times its size from multiple banks, all while betting on a few equities such as Viacom.[11] Not only were the targeted companies themselves leveraged, Archegos held total return swaps on the equities that were themselves funded by margin loans. Archegos blew up when Viacom decided to take advantage of its unrealistic equity price by issuing more shares. It thereby tanked its own equity price as markets realized the equity might be overvalued, prompting margin calls that Archegos could not meet, leading to further equity fire sales as banks sought to protect their positions. High asset prices and high leverage were clearly an unstable combination.

Debt that is supported by the cash flows generated by the borrowing entity is inherently safer, especially if the borrowing is long term. Debt that is supported by asset prices is inherently more fragile, yet quite widespread. In an economy with falling long-term interest rates stemming from accommodative policies, the rise in asset prices increases the equity value of borrowers, allowing them to borrow yet more. Moreover, as I argued in chapter 2, the prospect that other healthy players will be around to buy assets if a current borrower is unable to repay gives the borrower greater debt capacity. Debt capacity stems not from the cash flow the borrower generates but from the lenders' greater ability to sell the underlying assets to other players in the industry if the borrower defaults. The cycle is virtuous: greater debt capacity leads to higher bids for assets, which lead to greater equity among prospective buyers in the industry.

Of course, when rates rise, asset prices could fall, and the cycle could become a vicious one—prospective buyer equity falls, making potential buyers less able to buy at high prices, reducing the debt capacity of assets. The problem is compounded by the fact that, in times when borrowing based on prospective asset sale values is easy, both borrowers and lenders may neglect the underlying cash flows that will ultimately be needed to service debt when asset prices fall. The mortgage loans made prior to the GFC to borrowers with no income, no job, and no assets ("Ninja loans") came back to haunt lenders when house prices plummeted, and it was no longer possible to sell repossessed houses easily to recover amounts loaned. It is not difficult to see parallel forces at work in the red-hot market for private equity transactions today, raising concerns for the period when accommodation ends.

Liquidity Dependence

Central banks have been accommodative not just by keeping rates low but by expanding their balance sheets. The counterpart is an expansion in the central bank reserves held by commercial banks. Ordinarily, one would think that an expansion in the very liquid reserves should increase liquidity in the system. Yet the financial system has experienced severe liquidity shortages, both in September 2019 and March 2020, at times when reserves were four times what they were before the GFC.

The reality is that the supply of liquidity through reserves creates new demands for liquidity, sometimes exceeding the initial supply.[12] Specifically, commercial banks finance reserve holdings with wholesale deposits, which can turn into claims on liquidity in periods of stress. They also explicitly sell claims on liquidity such as committed credit lines. Regulators themselves want banks to set aside liquid assets to meet various regulatory ratios. Finally, if all these demands come due at the same time (and systemic stress tends to precipitate such correlated demands), some banks prefer to hoard liquidity, further exacerbating liquidity shortages. Of course, all this puts pressure on central banks to accommodate the stress by supplying yet more liquidity. To wean the system of such liquidity dependence is not easy, yet the prospect of an ever-expanding central bank balance sheet is also alarming, in part because of the consequences for fiscal health.

Balance Sheet Expansion and Fiscal Fragility

When the central bank buys long-term government debt and issues reserves (for instance, when engaging in QE), it effectively shortens the duration of the debt held by the public on the consolidated central bank/government balance sheets. Here is why: the central bank finances those purchases by borrowing overnight reserves from commercial banks on which it pays interest (also termed "interest on excess reserves"). From the perspective of the consolidated balance sheet of the government and the central bank (which, remember, is a wholly owned subsidiary of the government), the government has essentially swapped its long-term debt for overnight reserves placed with the banking system. QE thus drives a continuous shortening of effective government debt maturity and a corresponding increase in (consolidated) government and central bank exposure to rising interest rates.

Does this matter? Consider the fifteen-year average maturity of UK government debt. The median maturity is shorter, at eleven years, and falls to just four years when one accounts for the QE-driven shortening because of the government debt held by the Bank of England. A 1 percentage point increase in interest rates would therefore boost the UK government's effective interest payments by about 0.8 percent of GDP—which, the UK Office of Budget Responsibility notes, is about two-thirds of the medium-term fiscal tightening proposed over the same period. And, of course, rates could increase much more than 1 percentage point. In the case of the United States, not only is the outstanding government debt much shorter in maturity than that of the United Kingdom, but the Fed also owns one-quarter of it.

Ideally, the government would lengthen the maturity of the debt it issues, even as the central bank buys more, thus keeping the average effective maturity of the outstanding debt constant. This kind of coordination has not been seen. The broader point is that along with the expansion in public borrowing discussed earlier, the shortening of the duration of that borrowing exposes economies to the risk of fiscal fragility as rates move up.

Cross-Border Spillovers

Easy monetary policy in the core reserve countries leads to cross-border capital flows to periphery recipient countries. When the core countries tighten, capital flows back. The sensitivity of credit flows to US monetary policy is much greater in emerging markets and developing countries and is disproportionately focused on riskier emerging markets and riskier firms within.[13] To the extent that recipient countries are unprepared, given the phase of their business cycle or given the extent of borrowing, to accommodate outflows, stress spreads across borders. Since chapters 2 and 3 discuss monetary policy spillovers and the spillbacks (of reduced activity in recipient countries to core countries), I will confine myself to noting they could be sizable and that we need to consider whether these should be incorporated into monetary policy settings.

The Way Forward

So where do central banks go from here, given the impediments to acting and the costs of acting aggressively in a system that has become dependent on continued accommodation? Clearly, the temptation is to stay accommodative, hoping that inflationary pressures will die of their own accord. Yet inaction in the face of mounting evidence of the need for action will eventually be disruptive, perhaps even more so. Central banks have to recognize that the pandemic has changed the world in many ways, so they have to be data driven. At the same time, they do not have the luxury of waiting for certainty. They have to act firmly given their best interpretation of incomplete evidence, recognizing there are dangers of being aggressive as well as passive. The fragilities that have built up over the years of accommodative policy will not disappear and will have to be navigated. But as the world moves on, central banks should ask how we got here.

Populism and the Central Bank

Populism implies distrust in elite institutions, their objectives, and their operational decisions. According to the populist demagogue, tough policy choices are an elite conspiracy, intended by the elite to feather their nest while imposing pain on the masses. Central banks are the most elite of institutions, staffed by pointy-headed economists from elite institutions, speaking in an argot that only a chosen few understand. Central banks are easily caricatured by the demagogue.

There are then at least two ways of looking at central bank actions in recent years. Their actions could be seen as a laudable response to a stubbornly disinflationary environment. The untried unconventional policies are brave attempts to deliver on their mandates. The neglect of financial stability is partly a consequence of a limited set of central bank tools and the greater importance of reviving growth. This is the interpretation that most central bankers buy into.

There is a different diagnosis, however, perhaps dating from chairman Greenspan's failed attempt to talk down the market. It is that central banks have shied away whenever tough policies are required to deliver on their responsibility for monetary and financial stability, as they attempt to retain public approval in an increasingly fractured polity. While central banks are ostensibly independent, the resemblance of some of their policies to long-abandoned interventionist policies of the past is not coincidental. In this rendering, central banks have become more political, in line with the change in their societies. The truth probably lies in between.

Clearly, with their new instruments, central bankers have made the economy even more dependent on their actions. However, only time will establish whether these new instruments have aided macro-stability or created new sources of volatility. It certainly has made good central banking policy far more difficult, even as it has become far more critical for economic well-being. Perhaps that is the way central bankers want it!

What changes would I advocate? Almost surely, central banks have to pay more attention to financial stability. Clearly, they have to enhance their understanding here, as well as their supervisory and regulatory capabilities. If they were dozing when the risks to subprime lending built up, they have been in deep slumber as the cryptocurrency market has exploded. In the United States, macroprudential responsibility needs to be firmly allocated to one regulator, which should develop the capabilities to monitor and act or press relevant regulators to act.

The more difficult question is, how should monetary policy change? My belief is that it can do more by being more realistic in public communication about the limits of monetary policy and the dangers to financial stability of monetary policy overextension. However, since it is an evolving area of debate, perhaps it is best to end this chapter with questions, leaving my answers to the conclusion.

Questions That Need Answers

- What should the inflation mandate of central banks be? Should the mandate recognize that some aspects will be difficult to reach under certain conditions (e.g., higher inflation under disinflationary conditions)?

- What responsibility should the central bank have for financial stability? How should it choose between price stability and financial stability when the objectives conflict and macroprudential tools are likely to be ineffectual?

- Should central banks take on more responsibilities than just price and financial stability?

- Should central banks explain the limitations of their traditional tool box to the public, even at the risk of undermining faith in, and credibility of, central banks?

- What new tools are permissible? How much should central banks interfere in the functioning of markets beyond setting policy rates and auctioning liquidity? How much should their ability to intervene be constrained after every unprecedented intervention so that the market does not become dependent on the central bank?

- How much should central banks nod to public opinion? How do they retain their ability to take actions that may be necessary for long-run growth and stability but might result in unpopular pain in the short run?

Less Is More

As I write this, the much-feared inflation I referred to in the last chapter is upon us. Industrial country central bankers have fallen tremendously in the public's eyes. A short while ago, they were heroes, supporting feeble growth with unconventional monetary policies, promoting the hiring of minorities by allowing the labor market to run a little hot and even trying to hold back climate change, all while berating paralyzed legislatures to do more. Now they stand accused of botching their most important task, keeping inflation low and stable. Politicians, sniffing blood and mistrustful of unelected power, want to reexamine central bank mandates. Did central banks get it all wrong? If so, what should they do? In the last chapter, I examined what central banks did after the Global Financial Crisis. I will summarize the analysis here and draw implications for policy.

The Case for Central Bankers

Hindsight is, of course, 20/20. The pandemic was unprecedented and its consequences for the globalized economy very hard to predict. The fiscal response, perhaps much more generous because polarized legislatures could not agree on whom to exclude, was not easy to forecast. Few thought Vladimir Putin would go to war in February 2022, disrupting supply chains further and sending energy and food prices skyrocketing.

Undoubtedly, central bankers were slow to react to growing signs of inflation. In part, they believed they were still in the post-2008 financial crisis regime, when every price spike, even of oil, barely affected the overall price level. As described in chapter 4, in an attempt to boost excessively low inflation, the Fed even changed its framework during the pandemic, announcing it would be less reactive to anticipated inflation and would keep policies more accommodative for longer. This framework was appropriate for an era of structurally low demand and weak inflation but exactly the wrong one to espouse just as inflation was about to take off and every price increase fueled another. But who knew the times were a-changing?

Even with perfect foresight—and in reality, they are no better informed than capable market players—central bankers may still have been understandably behind the curve. A central bank cools inflation by slowing economic growth. Its policies have to be seen as reasonable or else it loses its independence. With governments having spent trillions to support their economies, employment just recovered from terrible lows, and inflation barely noticeable for over a decade, only a foolhardy central banker would have raised rates to disrupt growth if the public did not yet see inflation as a danger. Put differently, preemptive rate rises that slowed growth would have lacked public legitimacy—especially if they were successful and inflation did not rise subsequently. Central banks needed the public to see higher inflation to be able to take strong measures against it.

In sum, central bank hands were tied in different ways—by recent history and their beliefs, by the frameworks they had adopted to combat low inflation, and by the politics of the moment, with each of these factors influencing the other.

The Case Against

Yet stopping the postmortem at this point is probably overly generous to central banks. After all, their past actions reduced their room to maneuver and not just for the reasons just outlined. In particular, take the emergence of both fiscal dominance (whereby the central bank acts to accommodate the government's fiscal spending) and financial dominance (where the central bank acquiesces to the imperatives of the market). They clearly are not unrelated to central bank actions of the past few years.

Long periods of low interest rates and high liquidity prompt an increase in asset prices and associated leveraging. And both the government and the private sector levered up. Of course, the pandemic and Putin's war pushed up government spending. But so did ultra-low long-term interest rates and a bond market anesthetized by central bank actions such as quantitative easing. Indeed, there was a case for targeted government spending financed by long-term debt issues. Yet sensible economists making the case for spending did not caveat their recommendations enough, and fractured politics ensured that the only spending that could be legislated had something for everyone. And, of course, politicians, as always, drew on unsound but convenient theories (think Modern Monetary Theory) that gave them the license for unbridled spending.

Central banks compounded the problem by buying government debt financed by overnight reserves, thus shortening the

maturity of the financing of the consolidated balance sheet
of the government and the central bank. This means that as
interest rates rise, government finances, especially for slow-
growing countries with significant debt, are likely to become
more problematic. Fiscal considerations already weigh on the
policies of some central banks—for instance, the European
Central Bank worries about the effect of its monetary actions
on "fragmentation," the yields of debts of fiscally weaker
countries blowing out relative to the yields of stronger countries. At the very least, perhaps central banks should have recognized the changing nature of politics that made unbridled
spending more likely in response to shocks, even if they did
not anticipate the shocks. This may have made them more
concerned about suppressing long rates and espousing "low
for long" policy rates.

The private sector also levered up, both at the household
level (think Australia, Canada, and Sweden) and at the corporate level. But there is also a new, largely overlooked, concern—
liquidity dependence.[1] As the Fed pumped out reserves during
quantitative easing, commercial banks financed the reserves
largely with wholesale demand deposits, effectively shortening the maturity of their liabilities. In addition, in order to
generate fees off the large volume of low-return reserves sitting
on their balance sheets, they have written all sorts of liquidity promises to the private sector—committed lines of credit,
margin support for speculative positions (think of how much
banks were on the hook for rogue fund Archegos's speculative
positions), and so on. The problem is that as the central bank
shrinks its balance sheet, it is hard for commercial banks to
unwind these promises quickly. The private sector becomes
much more dependent on the central bank for continued

liquidity. We had a first glimpse of this in the UK pension turmoil in October 2022, which was diffused by a mix of central bank intervention and government back-tracking on its extravagant spending plans. The episode did suggest, however, a liquidity-dependent private sector that could potentially affect the central bank's plans to shrink its balance sheet to reduce monetary accommodation.

High asset prices, high private leverage, and liquidity dependence suggest the central bank could face financial dominance—where monetary policy responds to financial developments, such as a sharp fall in financial asset prices, rather than inflation. Regardless of whether it intends to be dominated or not, current private-sector forecasts that the Fed will be forced to cut policy rates quickly have made the Fed's task in removing monetary accommodation harder. It will have to be harsher for longer than it would want to be, absent these private-sector expectations. And that means greater adverse consequences to global activity. It also means that when asset prices reach their new equilibrium, households, pension funds, and insurance companies will all have experienced significant losses—and often, these are not the entities that benefited from the rise. The bureaucratically managed, the unsophisticated, and the relatively poor get drawn in at the tail end of an asset price boom, creating problematic distributional consequences that the central bank has some responsibility for.

Finally, one area where reserve country central bank policies have had effect but have had very limited consequences for their actions is on external spillovers (see chapter 3). Clearly, the policies of the core reserve countries affect the periphery, through capital flows and exchange rate movements. The periphery has to react, regardless of whether its policy actions are suitable for domestic conditions, failing which it suffers longer-term consequences such as asset price booms, excessive borrowing, and eventually debt distress. I will return to this issue shortly.

In sum, then, while central banks can make the case that they were surprised by recent events, they played a role in constraining their own policy space. With their asymmetric and unconventional policies, ostensibly intended to deal with the policy rate touching the lower bound, they have triggered a variety of imbalances that not only make fighting inflation harder but also create new problems for the world. Central banks are not innocent bystanders, and the fact that their role in precipitating the Global Financial Crisis was not adequately highlighted has given them a freedom of action that has resulted in new fragilities.

What Happens Now?

So what happens now? Central bankers know the battle against high inflation well and have the tools to combat it. They should be free to do their job. This is not a time for postmortems to assess central bank functioning.

But when central banks succeed in bringing inflation down, we will probably return to a low-growth world. It is hard to see what would offset the headwinds of aging populations, a slowing China, and a suspicious, militarizing, deglobalizing world. That low-inflation, low-growth world is one central bankers understand less well. The tools central bankers used after the financial crisis, such as quantitative easing, were not particularly effective in enhancing growth.[2] Furthermore, aggressive central bank actions could precipitate more fiscal and financial dominance.

A Fundamental Contradiction

So when all settles back down, what should central bank mandates look like? In matters such as combating climate change or promoting inclusion, the policies of central banks have only an indirect impact. Truly, these are tasks for governments. Central banks should not use the excuse of government paralysis to step into the breach.

But what about their mandate and their frameworks on monetary policy? The earlier discussion suggested a fundamental contradiction central banks face. Hitherto, there was a sense that they needed one framework—for instance, an inflation-targeting framework committing them to keep inflation within a band or symmetrically around a target. Yet as BIS General Manager Agustin Carstens argues, a low-inflation regime can be very different from a high-inflation regime.[3] Depending on the regime they are in, their framework may need to change. In a low-inflation regime, where inflation does not budge from low levels no matter the price shock, they may need to commit to being more tolerant of inflation in the future in order to raise inflation today. Put differently, as Paul Krugman argued, they have to commit to being rationally irresponsible. This means adopting policies and frameworks that effectively bind their hands, committing them to stay accommodative for long. But as argued above, this may precipitate regime change, for instance, by loosening perceived fiscal constraints.

Conversely, in a high-inflation regime, where every price shock propels more, central banks need a strong commitment to eradicate inflation at the earliest, following the mantra "when you stare inflation in the eyeballs, it is too late." The framework-induced commitment needed for the low-inflation regime is thus incompatible with the framework-induced commitment

needed for the high-inflation regime. But central banks cannot simply shift based on regime because they lose the power
of commitment. They may have to choose a framework for all
regimes.

Choosing Frameworks

If so, the balance of risks suggests they should reemphasize
their mandate to combat high inflation, using standard tools
like interest rate policy. What if inflation is too low? Perhaps like the virus, we should learn to live with it and avoid
tools like quantitative easing that have questionable positive
effects on real activity; distort credit, asset prices, and liquidity; and are hard to exit. Arguably, so long as low inflation
does not collapse into a deflationary spiral, central banks
should not fret excessively about it. Decades of low inflation
have not slowed Japan's growth or labor productivity, which
are more directly attributable to aging and a shrinking labor
force.

Central banks may also need a stronger mandate to maintain
financial stability—for an extended period of low inflation, as
we have seen, fuels higher asset prices and, consequently, leverage. Unfortunately, even though monetary theorists argue that
financial stability is best dealt with by macroprudential supervision, it has proven less than effective thus far—as evidenced by
the crypto bubble and house price booms. What about responsibilities for the external consequences of their policies? Central
bankers and academics should start a process of dialogue on
it, as suggested in chapter 3. For now, though, refocusing on
combating high inflation while maintaining financial stability
may be enough.

Will these twin mandates condemn the world to low growth? No, but they will place the onus for fostering growth back on the private sector and governments, where they belong. More focused and less interventionist central banks would probably deliver better outcomes than the high-inflation, high-leverage, low-growth world we now find ourselves in. For central banks, less may indeed be more.

Postscript: As I finish editing the proofs for this book, the financial sector fragilities that I worried about have started emerging. Two medium sized banks failed in the United States, all bank deposits were implicitly guaranteed, the Fed has started lending against the face value of eligible securities, while a large Swiss bank was hurriedly merged with another, with the support of government guarantees. The financial instability I warned about is with us. In the United States, the Fed and the Treasury are intervening to quell turmoil. Hopefully, instability will be contained, but it is too early to tell. All this suggests that the concerns expressed in this book are very real. We must rethink central bank policies if we are to return to strong, equitable, sustainable growth.

Notes

Introduction

1. See Rajan (2006).

2. A good introduction to her work is her Andrew Crockett Lecture, Rey (2017).

Chapter 1

1. Crockett (2001).

2. This summary updates an article I published in Rajan (2012).

3. Cowen (2011).

4. Streeck (2011).

5. See Hauptmeier, Sanchez-Fuentes, and Schuknecht (2011).

6. See Krishnamurthy (2010).

7. See, for example, Eggertsson and Krugman (2012).

8. If it went below zero, everyone would hold cash rather than place money in deposits yielding negative interest rates. Because there is a cost to holding a lot of cash (if nothing else, the insecurity), nominal interest rates have been reduced by some central banks to slightly below zero, but there is a limit to how low they can go.

9. I have tweaked the Eggertsson and Krugman (2012) model by introducing end-of-working-life savings behavior to get this result. Will the increase in asset prices as interest rates fall across the term structure compensate the saver? Possibly not if they tend to be risk averse and prefer safer assets such as CDs and bank deposits, where price appreciation is small relative to income.

10. See, for example, Bertrand and Morse (2016).

11. Mian and Sufi (2015).

12. Indeed, because the pattern of demand that is expressible has shifted with the change in access to borrowing, the pace at which the economy can grow without inflation may also fall. With too many construction workers and too few jewelers, greater demand may result in higher jewelry prices rather than more output.

13. For a related perspective, see King (2013).

14. The economic case is the classic argument associated with debt overhang (see Myers [1977] for the theory and Kroszner [2003] for evidence on the benefits to the United States of repudiating the gold clause backing debt in the 1930s).

15. Very targeted fiscal outlays, such as extended unemployment insurance in the affected areas, might also be effective, although they have other side effects.

16. Outright Monetary Transactions (OMT) is a program of the European Central Bank under which the bank makes purchases ("outright transactions") in secondary, sovereign bond markets, under certain conditions, of bonds issued by Eurozone member-states.

17. I draw on Bernanke, Reinhart, and Sack (2004); Borio and Disyatat (2009); and Woodford (2012) in this section.

18. But there is also evidence that attempts to influence either rate also prompts a reaction; corporations attempt to borrow in "cheaper" segments of the yield curve—segments that the government has vacated. See Stein, Greenwood, and Hanson (2010).

19. Another way of explaining the portfolio balance argument is that by taking risky longer-term bonds out of the portfolio of fixed-income

investors, they have greater unmet risk appetite, and the price of all risky assets, including remaining long-term bonds, will appreciate.

20. The Fed worried about deflation in the early stages of the crisis, but with inflationary expectations solidly anchored, this has become less of a concern.

21. One could ask how this differs from ordinary monetary policy. Forward guidance probably implies a commitment to low rates over a longer term than one would associate with more normal policy statements. Of course, over the past decade, the extraordinary has become the ordinary.

22. See, for example, Krishnamurthy and Vissing-Jorgensen (2011).

23. See Diamond and Rajan (2012) or Woodford (2012).

24. Krishnamurthy and Vissing-Jorgensen (2011).

> We evaluate the effect of the Federal Reserve's purchase of long-term Treasuries and other long-term bonds ("QE1" in 2008–2009 and "QE2" in 2010–2011) on interest rates. Using an event-study methodology that exploits both daily and intra-day data, we find a large and significant drop in nominal interest rates on long-term safe assets (Treasuries, Agency bonds, and highly-rated corporate bonds). This occurs mainly because there is a unique clientele for long-term safe nominal assets, and the Fed purchases reduce the supply of such assets and hence increase the equilibrium safety-premium. We find only small effects on nominal (default-adjusted) interest rates on less safe assets such as Baa corporate rates. The impact of quantitative easing on MBS rates is large when QE involves MBS purchases, but not when it involves Treasury purchases, indicating that a second main channel for QE is to affect the equilibrium price of mortgage-specific risk. Evidence from inflation swap rates and TIPS show that expected inflation increased due to both QE1 and QE2, implying that reductions in real rates were larger than reductions in nominal rates. Our analysis implies that (a) it is inappropriate to focus only on Treasury rates as a policy target because QE works through several channels that affect particular assets differently, and (b) effects on particular assets depend critically on which assets are purchased.

25. See Stein (2013). For evidence, also see, for example, Becker and Ivashina (2015); Ioannidou, Ongena, and Peydró (2009); Maddaloni and Peydró (2011). For the theory, see Diamond and Rajan (2012), Farhi and Tirole (2012), and Acharya, Pagano, and Volpin (2016).

26. See, for example, Adrian and Shin (2010), Adrian and Shin (2012), BIS (2011), Borio and Disyatat (2011), Cetorelli and Goldberg

(2012), Chudik and Fratzscher (2012), and Schularick and Taylor (2012).

27. See Rey (2013, 2017).

28. For a detailed analysis of the effects in a receiving country, see Barroso, da Silva, and Sales (2016).

29. See Caruana (2012) for reflections on this issue.

30. See, for example, Diamond and Rajan (2012) or Farhi and Tirole (2012).

31. See, for example, Cheng, Raina, and Xiong (2014).

32. For an interesting episode, see the farm mortgage crisis in the United States documented in Rajan and Ramcharan (2015).

Chapter 2

1. Diamond, Hu, and Rajan (2020a, 2020b).

2. See Eichenbaum and Evans (1995); Bruno and Shin (2015).

3. See Cesa-Bianchi, Ferrero, and Rebucci (2018) for the detailed evidence on currency appreciation and asset price growth around an international credit supply shock.

4. See, for example, Bruno and Shin (2015).

5. For a more detailed argument, see Borio and White (2004).

6. IMF (2012).

7. https://www.globalfinancialgovernance.org/

Chapter 3

1. The views represent those of the authors and not of the IMF or any of the institutions to which the authors belong.

2. See, for example, Taylor (2017) for evidence on the exchange rate consequences of unconventional monetary policy in recent years.

3. See, for example, Bernanke (2015).

4. See Alter and Elekdag (2020).

5. See Rey (2013); Baskaya et al. (2022); and Morais, Peydro, and Ruiz (2015).

6. See Shin (2016), for example, or chapter 2.

7. See Borio (2014b) and Borio and Disyatat (2009), for example.

8. One example of what could be rated green is the framework suggested by Taylor (2017), wherein countries would announce their rules-based monetary policies—with opt-outs in cases of emergency. Such a framework would have the added benefit of allowing countries to set reasonable reaction functions to source country policies.

9. See Svensson (2001).

10. See Mishra and Rajan (2019) for an overview.

11. See IMF (2006).

Chapter 4

1. See Geanakoplos (2010) for a related model.

2. See Greenspan (1996).

3. See Greenspan (2002).

4. As Mario Draghi (2012), the then ECB president put it, "Within our mandate, the ECB is ready to do whatever it takes to preserve the euro. And believe me, it will be enough." Indeed, just this statement seemed to be enough, and no OMT actions were actually undertaken.

5. See Tobin (1969).

6. See Krishnamurthy and Vissing-Jorgensen (2011).

7. Also see Cochrane (2018) and Greenlaw et al. (2018).

8. See, for example, Levy and Plosser (2022) and Plosser (2021).

9. See Coeure (2021).

10. See, for example, Rajan (2006).

11. See Smith (2021).

12. See Acharya and Rajan (2022).

13. See Brauning and Ivashina (2020).

Less Is More

1. See Acharya et al. (2022).

2. See, for example, Fabo et al. (2021).

3. See speech by Carstens (2022).

References

Acharya, Viral, Rahul Chauhan, Raghuram Rajan, and Sascha Steffens, 2022. Liquidity Dependence: Why Shrinking Central Bank Balance Sheets Is an Uphill Task, paper presented at the Federal Reserve Bank of Kansas City's Jackson Hole Symposium, Jackson Hole, WY, 27 August.

Acharya, Viral, Tim Eisert, Christian Eufinger, and Christian Hirsch, 2019. Whatever It Takes: The Real Effects of Unconventional Monetary Policy. *Review of Financial Studies* 32 (9): 3366–3411.

Acharya, Viral, and Raghuram Rajan, 2022. Liquidity, Liquidity Everywhere, Not a Drop to Use: Why Flooding Banks with Central Bank Reserves May Not Expand Liquidity, NBER Working Paper 29680.

Adrian, Tobias, and Hyun Song Shin, 2010. Liquidity and Leverage. *Journal of Financial Intermediation* 19:418–437.

Adrian, Tobias, and Hyun Song Shin, 2012. Procyclical Leverage and Value-at-Risk, Federal Reserve Bank of New York Staff Report 338. http://www.newyorkfed.org/research/staff_reports/sr338.html

Alter, Adrian, and Selim Elekdag, 2020. Emerging Market Corporate Leverage and Global Financial Conditions. *Journal of Corporate Finance* 62:101590. https://doi.org/10.1016/j.jcorpfin.2020.101590

Barroso, Joao, Luis Pereira da Silva, and Adriana Sales, 2016. Quantitative Easing and Related Capital Flows into Brazil, Measuring Its Effects and Transmission Channels through a Rigorous Counterfactual Evaluation. *Journal of International Money and Finance* 67:102–122.

Baskaya, Yusuf Soner, Julian di Giovanni, Sebnem Kalemli-Ozcan, and Mehmet Fatih Ulu, 2022. International Spillovers and Local Credit Cycles. *Review of Economic Studies* 89 (2): 733–773.

Becker, Bo, and Victoria Ivashina, 2015. Reaching for Yield in the Bond Market. *Journal of Finance* 70 (5): 1863–1902.

Bergant, Katharina, Prachi Mishra, and Raghuram Rajan, 2023, Cross-border Spillovers: How US Financial Conditions affect M&As Around the World, working paper, University of Chicago.

Bernanke, Ben S., 2015. Federal Reserve Policy in an International Context, paper presented at the 16th Jacques Polak Annual Research Conference, IMF, Washington, DC, 5–6 November.

Bernanke, Ben, Vincent Reinhart, and Brian Sack, 2004. Monetary Policy Alternatives at the Zero Lower Bound: An Empirical Assessment. *Brookings Papers on Economic Activity* 2004 (2): 1–100.

Borio, Claudio, 2014a. The Financial Cycle and Macroeconomics: What Have We Learnt? *Journal of Banking and Finance* 45:182–198.

Borio, Claudio, 2014b. The International Monetary and Financial System: Its Achilles Heel and What to Do about It, BIS Working Paper 456.

Borio, Claudio, and Piti Disyatat, 2009. Unconventional Monetary Policies: An Appraisal, BIS Working Paper 292.

Borio, Claudio, and Piti Disyatat, 2011. Global Imbalances and the Financial Crisis: Link or No Link? BIS Working Papers 346. http://www.bis.org/publ/work346.pdf

Borio, Claudio, and W. R. White, 2004. Whither Monetary and Financial Stability? The Implications of Evolving Policy Regimes (No. 147). Bank for International Settlements.

Brauning, F., and Ivashina, V., 2020. U.S. Monetary Policy and Emerging Market Credit Cycles. *Journal of Monetary Economics* 112:57–76.

Bruno, Valentina, and Hyun Song Shin, 2015. Capital Flows and the Risk-Taking Channel of Monetary Policy. *Journal of Monetary Economics* 71:119–132.

Calvo, Guillermo A., and Carmen M. Reinhart, 2002. Fear of Floating. *Quarterly Journal of Economics* 117 (2): 379–408.

Carstens, Agustin, 2022. The Return of Inflation. Speech at the International Center for Monetary and Banking Studies, Geneva, Switzerland, 5 April. https://www.bis.org/speeches/sp220405.pdf

Caruana, Jaime, 2012. Policy Making in an Inter-connected World, Federal Reserve Bank of Kansas City. http://www.kansascityfed.org/publications/research/escp/escp-2012.cfm

Cesa-Bianchi, Ambrogio, Andrea Ferrero, and Alessandro Rebucci, 2018. International Credit Supply Shocks. *Journal of International Economics* 112:219–237.

Cetorelli, Nicola, and Linda S. Goldberg, 2012. Banking Globalization and Monetary Transmission. *Journal of Finance* 67 (5): 1811–1843.

Cheng, Ing-Haw, Sahil Raina, and Wei Xiong, 2014. Wall Street and the Housing Bubble. *American Economic Review* 104 (9): 2797–2829.

Chudik, Alexander, and Marcel Fratzscher, 2012. Liquidity, Risk and the Global Transmission of the 2007–9 Financial Crisis and the 2010–11 Sovereign Debt Crisis, ECB Working Paper 1416.

Cochrane, J., 2018. Slok on QE, and a Great Paper. https://johnhcochrane.blogspot.com/2018/02/slok-on-qe-and-great-paper.html

Coeure, B., 2021. Finance Disrupted, speech at the 23rd Geneva Conference on the World Economy, Geneva, Switzerland, 7 October. https://www.bis.org/speeches/sp211007.htm

Cowen, T, 2011. *The Great Stagnation: How America Ate All the Low-Hanging Fruit of Modern History, Got Sick, and Will (Eventually) Feel Better: A Penguin eSpecial from Dutton.* New York: Penguin.

Crockett, Andrew, 2001. Monetary Policy and Financial Stability, BIS. http://www.bis.org/review/r010216b.pdf?frames=0

Di Maggio, Marco, Amir Kermani, and Christopher J. Palmer, 2020. How Quantitative Easing Works: Evidence on the Refinancing Channel. *Review of Economic Studies* 87 (3): 1498–1528.

Diamond, Douglas W., Yunzhi Hu, and Raghuram G. Rajan, 2020a. Pledgeability, Industry Liquidity, and Financing Cycles. *Journal of Finance* 75 (1): 419–461.

Diamond, Douglas W., Yunzhi Hu, and Raghuram G. Rajan, 2020b. The Spillovers from Easy Liquidity and the Implications for Multilateralism. *IMF Economic Review* 68 (1): 4–34.

Diamond, Douglas W., and Raghuram Rajan, 2012. Illiquid Banks, Financial Stability, and Interest Rate Policy. *Journal of Political Economy* 120 (3): 552–591.

Draghi, Mario, 2012. Speech by Mario Draghi, President of the European Central Bank at the Global Investment Conference, 26 July, London, UK. www.ecb.europa.eu/press/key/date/2012/html/sp120726.en.html

Eggertsson, Gauti B., and Paul Krugman, 2012. Debt, Deleveraging, and the Liquidity Trap: A Fisher-Minsky-Koo Approach. *Quarterly Journal of Economics* 127 (3): 1469–1513.

Eichenbaum, Martin, and Charles Evans, 1995. Some Empirical Evidence on the Effects of Shocks to Monetary Policy on Exchange Rates. *Quarterly Journal of Economics* 110 (4): 975–1009.

Eichengreen, B., M. El-Erian, A. Fraga, T. Ito, J. Pisani-Ferry, E. Prasad, R. Rajan, M. Ramos, C. Reinhart, H. Rey, D. Rodrik, K. Rogoff, H. S. Shin, A. Velasco, B. Weder di Mauro, and Y. Yu, 2011. Rethinking Central Banking, Report of the Committee on International Economic Policy and Reform. Washington, DC: Brookings Institution.

Fabo, Brian, Martina Jančoková, Elisabeth Kempf, and Ľuboš Pástor, 2021. Fifty Shades of QE: Comparing Findings of Central Bankers and Academics. *Journal of Monetary Economics* 120:1–20.

Farhi, Emmanuel, and Jean Tirole, 2012. Collective Moral Hazard, Maturity Mismatch, and Systemic Bailouts. *American Economic Review* 102:60–93.

Foley-Fisher, Nathan, Rodney Ramcharan, and Edison Yu, 2016. The Impact of Unconventional Monetary Policy on Firm Financing Constraints: Evidence from the Maturity Extension Program. *Journal of Financial Economics* 122:409–429.

Geanakoplos, John, 2010. The Leverage Cycle. *NBER Macroeconomic Annual* 24 (1): 1–65.

Gopinath, Gita, and Jeremy C. Stein, 2021. Banking, Trade, and the Making of a Dominant Currency. *Quarterly Journal of Economics* 136 (2): 783–830.

Greenlaw, David, James D. Hamilton, Ethan Harris, and Kenneth D. West, 2018. A Skeptical View of the Impact of the Fed's Balance Sheet. Chicago Booth Working Paper. https://research.chicagobooth.edu/-/me dia/research/igm/docs/2018-usmpf-report.pdf

Greenspan, Alan, 1996. The Challenges of Central Banking in a Democratic Society, speech at the American Enterprise Institute, Washington, DC, 5 December. www.federalreserve.gov/boarddocs/speeches /1996/19961205.htm

Greenspan, Alan, 2002. Opening Remarks. Federal Reserve Bank of Kansas City, Jackson Hole Conference, Jackson Hole, WY, 30 August.

Grosse-Rueschkamp, Benjamin, Sascha Steffen, and Daniel Streitz, 2019. A Capital Structure Channel of Monetary Policy. *Journal of Financial Economics* 133:357–378.

Hausmann, Ricardo, Ugo Panizza, and Ernesto Stein, 2001. Why Do Countries Float the Way They Float? *Journal of Development Economics* 66 (2): 387–414.

Hofmann, Boris, Hyun Song Shin, and Mauricio Villamizar-Villegas, 2019. FX Intervention and Domestic Credit: Evidence from High-Frequency Micro Data, BIS Working Paper 774.

International Monetary Fund, 2006. *Article IV of the Fund's Articles of Agreement: An Overview of the Legal Framework.* Washington, DC: International Monetary Fund.

International Monetary Fund, 2007. *Review of the 1977 Decision— Proposal for a New Decision, and Public Information Notice.* Washington, DC: International Monetary Fund.

International Monetary Fund, 2012. The Liberalization and Management of Capital Flows: An Institutional View. https://www.imf.org /external/np/pp/eng/2012/111412.pdf

Ioannidou, Vasso, Steven Ongena, and José Luis Peydró, 2009. Monetary Policy and Subprime Lending: A Tall Tale of Low Federal Funds Rates, Hazardous Loan and Reduced Loans Spreads. European Banking Centre Discussion Paper 45.

King, Mervyn, 2013. Monetary Policy: Many Targets, Many Instruments. Where Do We Stand? Remarks Given by the Governor of the Bank of England at the IMF Conference on Rethinking Macro Policy II: First Steps and Early Lessons, Washington, DC.

Kohn, Donald, 2015. Implementing Macroprudential and Monetary Policies: The Case for Two Committees, Speech at Federal Reserve Bank of Boston, Boston, MA. https://www.brookings.edu/on-the-record /implementing-macroprudential-and-monetary-policies-the-case-for -two-committees/

Krishnamurthy, Arvind, 2010. How Debt Markets Have Malfunctioned in the Crisis. *Journal of Economic Perspectives* 24 (1): 3–28.

Krishnamurthy, Arvind, and Annette Vissing-Jorgensen, 2011. The Effects of Quantitative Easing on Interest Rates: Channels and Implications for Policy. *Brookings Papers on Economic Activity* No. 2 (Fall): 215–265.

Kroszner, Randall, 2003. Is It Better to Forgive Than to Receive? An Empirical Analysis of the Impact of Debt Repudiation, Working Paper, University of Chicago.

Kydland, Finn E., and Edward C. Prescot, 1977. Rules Rather Than Discretion: The Inconsistency of Optimal Plans. *Journal of Political Economy* 85 (3): 473–492.

Levy, Mickey D., and Charles I. Plosser, 2022. The Murky Future of Monetary Policy. *Federal Reserve Bank of St. Louis Review*. https://doi .org/10.20955/r.104.178-88

Maddaloni, Angela, and José-Luis Peydró, 2011. Bank Risk Taking, Securitization, Supervision, and Low Interest Rates: Evidence from Lending Standards. *Review of Financial Studies* 24 (6): 2121–2165.

Mian, A., and A. Sufi, 2015. *House of Debt: How They (and You) Caused the Great Recession, and How We Can Prevent It from Happening Again.* Chicago, IL: University of Chicago Press.

Mishra, Prachi, and Raghuram Rajan, 2019. International Rules of the Monetary Game. In *Currencies, Capital, and Central Bank Balances*, edited by John Cochrane, Kyle Palermo, and John Taylor. Stanford, CA: Hoover Institution Press, 1–42.

Morais, Bernardo, José-Luis Peydro, and Claudia Ruiz, 2015. The International Bank Lending Channel of Monetary Policy Rates and QE: Credit Supply, Reach-for-Yield, and Real Effects. International Finance Discussion Papers 1137. Board of Governors of the Federal Reserve System.

Myers, Stewart, 1977. Determinants of Corporate Borrowing. *Journal of Financial Economics* 5:147–175.

Plosser, Charles, 2021. The Fed's Risky Experiment. Hoover Institution Working Paper 21116.

Rajan, Raghuram, 2006. Has Financial Development Made the World Riskier? *European Financial Management* 12 (4): 499–533.

Rajan, Raghuram, and Rodney Ramcharan, 2015. The Anatomy of a Credit Crisis: The Boom and Bust in Farm Land Prices in the United States in the 1920s. *American Economic Review* 105 (4): 1439–1477.

Rey, Helene, 2013. Dilemma not Trilemma: The Global Financial Cycle and Monetary Policy Independence, paper presented at the 25th Federal Reserve Bank of Kansas City Annual Economic Policy Symposium, Jackson Hole, WY, 24 August.

Rey, Helene, 2017. The Global Financial System, the Real Rate of Interest and a Long History of Boom-Bust Cycles, Andrew Crockett Memorial Lecture, Bank of International Settlements.

Rogoff, Kenneth, 1985. The Optimal Degree of Commitment to an Intermediary Monetary Target. *Quarterly Journal of Economics* 100:1169–1189.

Rogoff, Kenneth, 2004. Globalization and Global Disinflation. In Jackson Hole Symposium Proceedings, Monetary Policy and Uncertainty: Adapting to a Changing Economy, 77–112. Federal Reserve Bank of Kansas City. https://scholar.harvard.edu/files/rogoff/files/rogoff2003.pdf

Schularick, Moritz, and Alan M. Taylor, 2012. Credit Booms Gone Bust: Monetary Policy: Leverage Cycles, and Financial Crises, 1870–2008. *American Economic Review* 102:1029–1061.

Shin, Hyun Song, 2016. The Bank/Capital Markets Nexus Goes Global, speech given at the London School of Economics and Political Science, London, UK, 15 November.

Smith, Annabel, 2021. KBC AM Fixed Income Dealer Departs for Tradeweb Product Development Role. The Trade. https://www.thetradenews.com/kbc-am-fixed-income-dealer-departs-for-tradeweb-product-development-role/.

Stein, Jeremy C., 2013. Overheating in Credit Markets: Origins, Measurement, and Policy Responses, Board of Governors of the Federal Reserve System. http://www.federalreserve.gov/newsevents/speech/stein20130207a.htm.

Stein, Jeremy, Robin Greenwood, and Samuel Hanson, 2010. A Gap-Filling Theory of Corporate Debt Maturity Choice. *Journal of Finance* 65 (3): 993–1028.

Streeck, Wolfgang, 2011. The Crises of Democratic Capitalism. *New Left Review.* https://newleftreview.org/issues/ii71/articles/wolfgang-streeck-the-crises-of-democratic-capitalism.

Svensson, Lars E. O., 2001. The Zero Bound in an Open Economy: A Foolproof Way of Escaping from a Liquidity Trap. *Monetary and Economic Studies* 19 (S-1): 277–312.

Taylor, John B., 1993. Discretion versus Policy Rules in Practice. In *Carnegie-Rochester Conference Series on Public Policy* (Vol. 39, 195–214). Amsterdam: North-Holland.

Taylor, John B., 2017. Ideas and Institutions in Monetary Policy Making, the Karl Brunner Lecture, Swiss National Bank, Zurich, Switzerland, 21 September.

Tobin, James, 1969. A General Equilibrium Approach to Monetary Theory. *Journal of Money, Credit and Banking* 1 (1): 15–29.

Woodford, Michael, 2012. Methods of Policy Accommodation at the Interest-Rate Lower Bound, paper presented at the Federal Reserve Bank of Kansas City Symposium at Jackson Hole, Jackson Hole, WY, 31 August.

Index